In Search of the King

Annell Williamson

ISBN: 978-1-105-08601-4

For My Children

A Special Thanks

This story could not have been written without the involvement of my husband, Glen who brought the characters to life through illustration, my children, for whom the story was written, and my two wonderful sisters who encouraged me along the way.

–Annell Williamson

Forward

By Cory Williamson

"Every good gift and every perfect gift is from above, and cometh down from the Father..." —James 1:17

One night my mother had a dream about a rag-tag group of animals on the streets of Jerusalem. Despite their many differences, the animals banded together to complete a mission to save a newborn child from a wicked king. The meaning of the dream wasn't completely clear at the time, but the feeling of the dream so affected her that she felt compelled to capture it for her children.

But dreams are funny things. They don't arrive as edited prose, written with perfect syntax and complete with chapter headings. Instead, from inception, dreams arrive as bursts of imagery, with characters imperceptibly slipping on and off the stage of the subconscious mind. Dreams are a kaleidoscope of impressions that must be interpreted and augmented in order to derive meaning. And so it was with this dream.

Mom worked on the story for quite some time. It became a labor of love. She wrote and revised. She studied ancient Israel, its customs, its people, its animals, and its architecture. She pored over scripture and other religious texts to learn everything she could learn to fill in the gaps of her dream.

During that time, the setting became more authentic, the plot more intriguing, and the characters more compelling. The result is a wonderful story that comes to life through the hearts and eyes of some very special animals that we get to know and love.

As much as this story is a gift from a loving mother to her children, it is also a gift from a loving Heavenly Father to His children. It is a story about what it means to go "in search of the King…" how to find Him, and how each of us can receive the greatest gift of all.

PART
1

1

Nazareth to Jerusalem

As the little donkey Heber rested inside his lean-to, the first light of dawn peered over the hills into the fertile valley of Nazareth. The young carpenter, Joseph, would be returning soon to finish arranging the panniers on Heber's back. Joseph had risen before daylight to start preparation for the journey to Jerusalem. From a neighboring rooftop Ezra, Nazareth's oldest rooster, cleared his throat and announced with a raspy crow, that morning had finally arrived in Nazareth. Now that there was enough daylight to travel, the caravan would be leaving for the city.

Naomi, a plump hen that lived next door but often visited Heber to entertain him with her numerous questions and gossip, fluttered off her perch. She hurried to Heber's tiny shelter. As she strutted in a circle around him her prying eyes curiously observed Heber's heavily laden panniers.

"Heber," she clucked, "where are you going?"

Heber pretended not to hear.

"Did you hear me? I want to know where you are going," she demanded.

Heber gave a slow, gaping yawn. Swatting his tail at an annoying fly that had also begun its day with the rising of the sun, he remained silent.

"Speak to me, you dumb animal!" Naomi chirped. "I want to know where you are going."

Heber continued to ignore her demands. He refused to give her any information that could be told to the rest of the gossiping hens in Nazareth.

"Well, I hope you are not going to Jerusalem," Naomi said smugly. "News is King Herod has angered the Jewish people. He is hosting the Roman games and plans to invite Caesar Augustus so he can entertain him with this elaborate celebration." Naomi paused for a moment to see if Heber was listening. "You know these games are dedicated to the worship of Roman gods. If you ask me I think they are too costly and violate all of our people's religious beliefs. Herod has certainly overtaxed his Jewish subjects so he can furnish himself with that huge palace full of gold, marble, fine furniture, servants, and worst of all, his concubines. I'm sure he is determined to impress Caesar when he arrives at Jerusalem for the games." Naomi hesitated for a moment as she took a deep breath, and then continued. "I've heard by the way side, there is sure to be a rebellion. If I were there I would rebel too. Wouldn't you?"

Heber pretended to doze as Naomi droned on. He wished she would go back to her own yard.

"The rumors of a rebellion have alerted the Romans," informed Naomi. "They say people are getting arrested everyday for no reason at all. Jerusalem is not a safe place. I certainly would not want to go there right now. Would you?"

Heber refused to answer her.

Naomi moved closer to Heber and talked louder. "I think Herod is a wicked lunatic! The story is, in one of his fits of anger, he had his wife Mariamne arrested. He accused her of plotting against him, and she was executed for treason. Now he can't close his eyes without seeing her. They claim he loved her more than any of his other wives. It would be better to be his royal cat than his family!"

Heber glanced at Naomi. She had a terrified look in her eyes.

"You've heard about his cat haven't you?" she asked.

Heber had not heard anything about Herod's cat and he did not want Naomi to tell him about the cat. He was already tired of listening to her. However it was obvious she was not going to leave without telling him about Herod's cat.

Naomi moved closer to Heber and in a slow whisper she said, "They say this rare caracal cat was a gift from one of his wives and has been trained to hunt small game for Herod. It's been told the cat is 50 pounds of muscle, claws and teeth and is a merciless killer. He has been known to take down prey twice his size. I'm sure all the animals in Jerusalem live in fear of this night predator." Naomi looked Heber straight in the eye, "I think Herod and his cat are nasty and downright malicious, don't you?" She raised her wing to her forehead and groaned, "How much longer must we suffer under the rule of this Roman scum with Herod as our king? We need a new king!"

Heber, who was determined to remain silent, hoped Joseph would return soon so Naomi would leave.

Naomi glared at Heber. "I declare, you are the most stubborn animal I know. You drive me absolutely mad with your silence," she huffed. "Why won't you talk to me? You are such a dull creature. I can see I'm wasting my words on a nitwit." Naomi turned her back and wiggled her tail feathers at Heber. "I am leaving! Good-bye," she grumbled.

Just then, Joseph with his arms full of supplies, hurried across the courtyard toward Heber. When he nearly stepped on Naomi, the hen scolded him with a series of frenzied clucks. Heber gave a sigh of relief as he watched Naomi's tail feathers disappear into the distance.

Joseph rushed into the lean-to. He loaded nutmeats, olive cakes, bags of water, a few dried figs, and other provisions into

In Search of the King

Heber's panniers. These would be needed for the long journey to Jerusalem. He checked Heber's panniers one last time, and then quickly untied Heber's lead rope. Heber followed Joseph as they hurried out into the courtyard to join the caravan. Heber looked up and there stood the beautiful young Mary before him. Mary's blue linen frock extended nearly to the ground. It was gathered at the waist by a braided cloth sash. Her brown tunic hung loosely over her frock. A veil covered her head and dropped down her back. "Joseph—" she began worriedly-but Joseph interrupted.

"I know what you are going to say, Mary."

Mary hesitated for a moment before continuing. "Jerusalem is not a safe place to be right now."

Joseph took Mary's hand, "You must not worry. We both know that I must go. We've been betrothed for nearly a year. With my carpenter skills, I can get employment in the city and quickly save enough money to pay the dowry, so we can be married.

"Please, Joseph, be careful," she said. "Peace to you."

"While we are apart for this short time, Mary, I wish peace to you as well. I—"

"Joseph, Joseph! Hurry!" interrupted Joseph's friend Phillip.

Joseph's friends Phillip and Daniel were also going to the Holy City Jerusalem to seek temporary employment.

"The caravan is leaving. You must come now!" added Daniel.

Joseph smiled at Mary then hurried toward his friends in the caravan. "I won't be long," he shouted over his shoulder.

As Joseph and the rest of the caravan passed over the first hill leading out of Nazareth, Heber glanced back to see Mary still standing in the courtyard watching them leave. Joseph turned and waved good-bye to her.

2

The Throne Room

The royal cat, Felix, felt the fur on the back of his neck bristle. He twitched his black tufted ears and listened closely. Footsteps advanced from outside. Suddenly, the huge cedar doors flew open and crashed against the wall.

"A rebellion could ruin me!" shrieked King Herod as he burst into the room.

Several guards followed Herod into the room. Felix flattened his ears against his head, hissed and then slowly inched backward seeking a hiding place behind the king's throne. Felix was accustomed to Herod's fits of rage and had learned to stay away from him at times like this. He riveted his eyes on Herod as the king paced back and forth across the room screaming at the guards.

"I am highly regarded by the Roman Emperor, Caesar Augustus. That is the reason he has chosen me, king of the Jews. I have maintained peace for a long time. I have gained great riches. If I am to secure my position, I must keep these people obedient and under control!" When Herod slammed his fist onto the table, Felix jumped and moved further behind Herod's throne.

"I cannot risk a rebellion!" Herod screamed. "Why are they opposing me on these games?"

The guards stood in silence, afraid to speak. After a short time Herod paused. His eyes narrowed as he stroked his beard. Staring at the floor, he mumbled, "I will do whatever it takes to remain king."

In Search of the King

Finally he motioned for the guards to leave the throne room. Felix watched Herod closely as he walked to a small cupboard in the corner of the room. Reaching in, Herod pulled out his favorite amphora of wine and poured some into a silver cup. Herod walked back to his throne. He folded his scarlet robe around himself then sat and relaxed. He raised the cup of wine to his lips and slowly took a sip—then another and another. Once Herod had been described as a man of great bravery and skilled marksmanship. Now there were whisperings in the palace that he was an old wine bibber. Yet even in his deteriorating state he held the power in Judea.

The dark circles underneath his eyes revealed his lack of rest. The wine seemed to soothe Herod's nerves and after a short time, he fell asleep.

Felix moved back to his usual place at the base of Herod's throne. He preened himself with strokes of his tongue. He could feel the warmth of the morning sun that filtered through the east window of the palace. He took pleasure in the luxurious life at the palace. However, sometimes he would long for the freedoms he possessed as a wild caracal living in the wilderness. Now, trained to hunt small game for the king he was proud to be known as the royal caracal. The jeweled collar that hung around his neck and the silver serving dish were gifts from the king when he had performed at his best.

Suddenly Herod jolted upright. "Mariamne, Mariamne!" he screamed.

Felix quickly moved back behind the throne again. Herod banged the chimes and instantly a stout hardy young man appeared. "Tell Mariamne I want to speak to her concerning this trouble in Jerusalem," he ordered.

"Your majesty..." the messenger hesitated before he spoke. "Do you not remember? Mariamne is no longer with us."

Herod's eyes grew cold and angry. Without warning he threw his wine cup at the young man. The messenger leaped aside and the cup crashed against the wall with a bang.

Quivering with rage, Herod exclaimed, "I know she is not here, you fool!"

Felix startled by the outburst jumped and moved deeper into the shadows. The messenger stood frozen in place. Herod leaned over and put his head down in his hands. After a few moments he raised his head and a smile spread across his face. He stood and walked to a table on the opposite side of the room. On the table was a scroll. Herod carefully wrote a message on the scroll and handed it to the messenger.

"Take this order and deliver it to those in the court of the Sanhedrin," Herod commanded. "They are to report to me at once."

3

The Sanhedrin

Later in the day, Felix took his place next to Herod's throne as members of the Sanhedrin gathered at the palace. Chief priests, rabbis, scribes, Sadducees, and Pharisees came dressed in their finest clothes to meet with Herod. Felix had seldom been in the same room with so many members of the Jewish court, the Sanhedrin, the most rich and influential men in Jerusalem.

Herod stood to greet them. "My dear friends," Herod said with a wave of his arm, "I have invited you here today to address your concerns regarding the Roman Olympiad games I am bringing to Jerusalem. I have not ignored your needs in these difficult times. My duties as king to build up Jerusalem have brought you more security. I will do what I can to help us regain our freedom from this Roman bondage," he promised. His eyes narrowed. "Remember, I too am a Jew." Herod motioned to his servants to pour his guests some wine. "I have been nothing but a friend to you. You must trust me. By honoring Caesar with these games, we will gain his approval and our people will be allowed to prosper."

The sound of contentious murmuring filled the room. An old rabbi stood and stepped forward. His long white beard hung in soft curls down the front of his robe. When he lifted his head to speak, the chatter stopped. "These games will prosper no one," he argued.

Herod scowled, "May I remind you once again what I have done for Jerusalem?" he said. He looked directly at the old rabbi. "I have advanced in every way the nation of the Jews." Herod stepped away from his throne and walked toward the window. "By God's will I am your king, and since I have prospered so greatly, I give thanks to our God for giving me this kingdom. I, Herod, have worked diligently to rebuild our temple." He pointed out the window to the magnificent structure that towered above Jerusalem. "When it is finished, it will be much larger and more beautiful than ever before! No one has so greatly adorned the temple as I. My plans to complete the temple and add more walls will fortify the city for our protection."

The old rabbi folded his arms across his chest and in a deep voice answered. "You claim to be a Jew, but by bringing this celebration to Jerusalem you are asking your own people to approve games dedicated to the worship of Roman gods. By asking us to change our laws, and accept the corrupt practices of foreign countries, you will bring the wrath of God upon us."

With his fist clenched, Herod turned and faced the rabbi. He cried out in frustration, "Why must you oppose me? This is nonsense! Forget your silly superstitions and progress with me. If you cannot, then I suggest you hold your tongue."

"I am not finished," said the rabbi. "In the name of progress you have burdened our people with heavy taxes. You take our holy money from the temple and build elaborate structures for yourself in which you plan to entertain rich leaders from other nations."

Herod's eyes darkened, but the rabbi continued. "We are concerned with the wild animals your men have been gathering. We are aware of your intentions. Must we remain silent while the condemned men of Jerusalem will be required to fight lions, bears, and hyenas, only to be killed and devoured by the beasts? It is a hideous deed to watch men die for the delight of others."

"They are condemned men who will die anyway," Herod said. "They are no better than the animals they will fight!"

Again, from behind the beard came the confident voice of the rabbi. "The supreme law of Judaism is to respect one's life and death. They should not be executed for public amusement."

Instantly, a young scribe stood and joined the rabbi. "Is it true you are planning to take our sacred doves and use them for blood and sport in the arena of the caracal cats?" he asked. Herod stared at the young man, but refused to answer. Felix was looking forward to this event. He had been specifically trained for the contest and was expected to win.

The scribe continued to question Herod. "What about the gladiators that will be required to fight to the death? These acts are bloody and accursed in the sight of the Lord. We cannot allow these games to come to Jerusalem. Many lives will be uselessly lost in the savage brutality of these events!"

Herod turned and with his hard, squinty eyes looked directly at the scribe. Wiping the corner of his mouth with his sleeve he whispered, "It would be so unfortunate if your life was the first to be lost."

The scribe returned to his place and sank down in his seat.

Herod smiled. "You all are powerful leaders in this community," he said. "You are influential. You are wealthy. You have families that you love. If you value any of these things, let go of your ridiculous beliefs and convince the rest of our people to do the same."

When the rabbi took a step closer toward Herod, Felix flattened his ears against his head, hissed at the old rabbi, and took a firm swipe at him. Lucky for the rabbi he missed.

The rabbi continued his argument with Herod. "You are encouraging these barbaric rituals by promising golden trophies and great rewards to the winners," he said. "You have decorated Jerusalem with monuments to Caesar and images of the Romans' pagan gods. By doing this, you are demanding we worship images that are unworthy before our God. We refuse to worship such images. To anger our God could bring about our destruction."

The rest of the leaders nodded in agreement. Felix knew nothing of the anger of the rabbi's God but he knew what it meant to anger Herod. The men of the Sanhedrin were powerful men but Herod was more powerful. To anger Herod could mean destruction for those who opposed him.

"I am a generous man," scoffed Herod. "Great rewards will be offered to those of you who help me keep peace in the land."

The rabbi's eyes revealed his disgust for the king. "Are you going to force us with your bribery to accept and teach customs that violently betray God's laws?" he questioned.

Herod motioned to the door. "Go back to your homes and speak of Herod's kindness."

The men stood and began to leave the room. The rabbi cried out to them. "Stop! You do not understand! This is blasphemy! You are making a horrible mistake. Our spiritual well-being is more important than any earthly empire."

Herod motioned to several of the nearby guards, "Arrest this man!" He ordered. "I'll not stand for such acts of treason in my palace!"

Herod's guards immediately seized the old rabbi. Before they could escort him out of the room the rabbi faced Herod once again and said, "What will we be judged on? Will our God look at all our awards and trophies?"

"Herod yelled at the guards, "Get him out of here.""

After everyone had left, Herod sat down in his throne. Herod leaned back and smiled. "There will be no rebellion," he whispered to himself as he stroked Felix's head.

Felix had just begun to savor a moment of rest when one of the palace guards returned and announced a visitor.

"How dare anyone interrupt me without being invited!" snarled Herod.

"Your Majesty, it is the Roman centurion Balbus. He has been sent from the Antonia Fortress to speak to you."

Immediately, Herod regained his composure before he spoke, "Present him to me then."

The guard opened the doors and stood aside for Balbus to enter. The large centurion, clothed in his red uniform and silver mail approached Herod with confidence. The Roman's muscular body and attire marked him as a leader and a mighty warrior.

Herod greeted Balbus with a forced smile. "What brings me the pleasure of your company?" he asked.

The Roman's face, scarred from the wounds of a vicious battle, was stern as he spoke. "There have been rumors of a rebellion.

The procurator is wondering if we need to have more troops sent from Caesarea to keep these rebels under your control."

"Certainly not," answered Herod. "We should not bother Caesar with such trivial matters. I know how to deal with my people." Herod stood up, took several gold coins from his treasury, and handed them to Balbus. "Go back to your post and report that I have this situation under control," he said.

Without emotion, Balbus answered, "Consider it done."

The centurion's red cloak flowed behind him as he quickly turned and marched away.

4

Joseph Meets Lydia

The journey had been long from Nazareth to Jerusalem. Heber's legs ached, but finally the weary travelers reached the city. Other caravans were already there, and traders were selling all sorts of wares. Heber did not envy their camels, packed with heavy merchandise. He thought his load felt heavy, but the camels groaned and swayed beneath the loads they were made to bear. Still, the marketplace seemed to be a bustling, happy place. Brightly colored cloth, fruit and vegetables, clay pots and jugs lined the displays. Baskets hung overhead in many of the stands in the marketplace. Craftsmen worked their trades while children played games in the streets. Daniel, Phillip, and Joseph were not the only ones who had come to Jerusalem, hoping to find employment during the building of Herod's temple.

Joseph led Heber slowly through the marketplace. Suddenly, the chatter of the marketplace was shattered by an angry cry. Heber looked in the direction of the startling outburst and saw a man jumping up and down, clutching his backside in a most peculiar fashion.

"Lydia!" the man shouted in a nasal, high-pitched voice, "If you bite me one more time I'll carve you up and feed you to the dogs!"

The dispute between the camel and her owner began to attract some attention. Heber followed Joseph and his friends as they joined the growing crowd. The midday sun was growing hotter by the minute and so was the camel owner's temper. Beads of sweat ran down his forehead and dripped off the end of his long, beaked nose. With a stick in his hand, he approached the camel cautiously. He walked slowly around the sullen animal, trying to sneak up on her without getting bitten. The camel's fierce eyes followed every move her master made. When the man raised his hand to strike her, the camel spit her cud at him and it hit him in the face. The man immediately went into violent fits of coughing and gagging. Waving his stick like a sword, he attacked in full force against the camel. She blocked him with her hind leg and sent him flying through the air.

"I think this man is in need of help," said Joseph. "We'd better do something."

Daniel disagreed sharply. "Not me. I'd rather fight the Roman army than that belligerent beast."

"Well, I am going to see if I can do something to end this dispute," Joseph insisted.

Phillip grabbed him by the arm. "Remember, Joseph, there are only two ways to handle a camel."

"And nobody knows either of them," joked Daniel.

Joseph stepped forward, helped the camel's owner to his feet and asked. "May I be of some help, sir?"

The man's hands flailed in the air, "I can't get this ugly, ill-tempered nuisance to budge. She's as untamed as the desert itself." With that, he slumped over, put his head in his hands, and began to make horrible sobbing noises.

Heber looked at Joseph, then at the camel. She was rather large. She had big eyes with long eyelashes, a droopy lower lip, and a tuft of hair that sprang up between her ears. Heber could see from the look in her eyes that she had no intention of doing anything that her owner wanted.

As Joseph approached the camel he began talking to her in soothing tones. "Why are you being so contrary? Has some one offended you?"

The camel's dark eyes softened.

Joseph turned to Daniel. "This is a beautiful camel," he said.

"Yes," agreed Daniel, "I've noticed. Her legs are her most striking feature."

Joseph reached in his leather scrip and pulled out a handful of dried figs. He carefully offered them to Lydia. She nuzzled them cautiously with her lips and then devoured them.

"She seems to have a passion for dried figs," chuckled Joseph. He cautiously walked around the sullen camel. Suddenly, he stopped. "Here is the problem," Joseph said. "I believe someone has not treated you very kindly." Then turning toward the man he explained, "She is in pain. You've cinched her too tightly and the girth has made a sore on her side. It's easy to understand why she does not want to move."

With his hands still covering his face, the man peered between his fingers at Joseph.

As Joseph gently loosened the girth on the saddle, Lydia swung her head around as if she might bite. Joseph stopped and handed her a few more dried figs. Once the girth was loosened, Joseph took a piece of cloth from Heber's panniers and placed it between the girth and the sore on Lydia's side.

"There," Joseph told the owner. "See if that makes her a little more cooperative."

The man stood up and moved slowly toward Lydia. He warily took hold of her bridle reins. Then he smacked his stick on the ground and commanded her to kneel. Lydia dropped to her knees and then to her side. Cautiously, the man swung his right leg over the camel's back and settled himself in the saddle. With a groan, the large animal heaved to her feet. Her deafening bellows caused the crowd to scatter.

There was a moment of silence, then Lydia bolted.

The man clung to the reins as his head jerked backward and he nearly bounced out of the saddle. "Whoa! Stop! Whoooooa!" he cried as he tried to gain control of the fleeing camel, but Lydia continued galloping at full speed out of the marketplace, complaining bitterly the whole way.

Joseph looked in amazement at his friends. Daniel shrugged his shoulders, "At least you got her to move."

5

Baruch and the Beggar

Heber followed Joseph and his friends through the marketplace as they continued to inquire where they might find work. Several times they stopped and asked information from some of the merchants. Near one of the merchants' stands Heber noticed a beggar near the edge of the cobbled street, sitting in the shadows of a brick building. With his hands outstretched, he begged for alms. His clothing was not much more than shreds. He wore layers of rags on his feet, and in his fist he clutched a gnarled walking stick. A scruffy looking dog lay curled up next to him. The dog's brown and gray hair was long and matted in clumps against his body. He lifted his head and sniffed the air. Maybe he was searching for a hand out. His gaunt belly looked like it had been awhile since he had had a morsel of food.

As Joseph led Heber toward the beggar the dog fastened a cold eye on Joseph. Joseph approached the beggar with caution. "Hello," he whispered.

At first the beggar cowered deeper into the shadows, but then he slowly turned his head and his sightless, cloudy eyes searched for the person who had spoken to him. "Who is there?"

"I am Joseph of Nazareth." Joseph reached into Heber's panniers and took a fig cake, and some goat cheese and placed the food in the beggar's hand.

"Bless you," he said.

In Search of the King

The beggar slowly broke off a small portion of the cake and shared it with the scrawny dog. "Here, Baruch," he said. The dog carefully took the cake from the beggar and devoured it.

Suddenly, a hush came over the marketplace as the sound of horse hooves was heard approaching on the cobbled street. Heber could hear the terrified whisperings from the crowd, "It's Balbus."

He looked up to see a scar-faced centurion riding toward them on a light grey stallion.

Following behind on foot were several more Roman soldiers. Heber wanted to move from the path of the Roman troops but Joseph stood firm.

"Joseph," Daniel said as he grabbed Joseph's arm, "They are coming toward us."

"We have no need to fear," Joseph said. "We have broken no law."

Balbus stopped and dismounted. He pulled a scourging whip from his belt. Heber's legs trembled as the captain took long strides toward them. The captain shoved Joseph aside. Balbus pulled back the whip and yelled, "Caesar will soon arrive here. We will not have such lice-infested beggars cluttering our streets." The crack of the scourging whip was followed by a cry of agony from the beggar.

Heber could see that part of the beggar's tunic was torn from his shoulders by the stinging tongues of the whip. In an instant, the dog Baruch leapt at Balbus and sunk his teeth deep into the captain's leg. Balbus struck the dog and sent him rolling across the cobbled street, where he lay motionless. The poor beggar tried crawling to safety but Balbus inflicted another blow across the beggar's back tearing more of his clothing and flesh.

Joseph dropped Heber's lead rope and ran to help the beggar. Exposing his own back, Joseph bent over to lift the beggar. Then came another sharp cracking sound. Joseph groaned and fell to his knees.

Daniel and Phillip moved toward him, but were blocked by the drawn swords of Balbus' soldiers. Joseph struggled to his feet and lifted the beggar with him.

Baruch finally regained his senses and snapping and snarling came again to attack Balbus. Balbus turned to face the angry dog. Baruch stayed out of reach of the Centurion's blows. He was able to distract Balbus long enough for Joseph and the beggar to disappear between two merchant stands.

Balbus turned and tried to follow them, but Heber kicked the corner pole of the nearby stand and the goat-hair awning dropped on Balbus.

A moment of banging and cursing followed and then an angry Balbus emerged from the rubble, covered with bits of fruit and Jewish clothing. The marketplace erupted in laughter.

"Get out of my way!" Balbus snarled as he shoved another merchant aside and mounted his horse. He immediately rode from the marketplace, his vassal of soldiers followed after him.

Joseph returned shortly to find his friends. His act of kindness had found safety for the beggar and allowed the dog Baruch enough time to escape. Cheers from the crowd welcomed Joseph's presence, but Phillip was not cheering. He shook his fist at Joseph. "You risked your life for that beggar!" he scolded. "You could have been killed. You took a chance with your life— and ours—to save him!"

"Are we not all beggars?" Joseph asked. "Do we not all pray to the same God for our well-being?"

Phillip hung his head, hesitated for a moment, and then looked up. "I'm sorry," he answered. "I guess you are right, Joseph. As the Lord's people, we have always been commanded to serve one another."

"You did the right thing," assured Daniel. Then he added with a smile, "It does my heart good to see those Romans humbled once in a while."

Joseph gave Heber a pat on the neck. "Thanks, my little friend," he said.

Joseph placed his hand on Phillip's shoulder. Pointing to the bewildered merchant he said, "Let us help this man repair the damage that has been done."

While they were putting the merchant's stand back together, a burly fellow approached Joseph. An immense beard of coarse red hair covered most of his face. "My name is Zebedee," the man said as he shook Joseph's hand. "I hear you are looking for work."

"We have traveled here from Nazareth hoping to find employment," Joseph answered.

"Meet me at Herod's quarry on the morning of the New Moon's Day. I think I can help you." He nodded at Joseph and turned to continue on his way.

Joseph called out to Zebedee as he started to leave. "Do you know where we can find a place to stay?"

"Go to the lower city. Ask for Jabin. He can help you. Tell him Zebedee sent you."

"I also need a place to rest my donkey. Where might I lodge him for the night?"

"On the south end of Mt. Ophel just outside the city wall there is a stable. It belongs to me," said Zebedee. "You will find a boy there. Tell him I sent you. He will care for the donkey."

"Thank you," said Joseph.

Joseph and his friends had scarcely finished putting the merchant stand back together when they heard the sound of trumpets, cymbals, and music in the distance. When Joseph looked up he saw Balbus riding toward them.

"Move aside! Move aside," Balbus commanded. "Caesar is coming through."

Balbus cleared the way for the Roman emperor to pass. To avoid the sting of the whip, people pushed against the buildings. Fearing another confrontation, Joseph quickly led Heber away from the street and disappeared into the crowd. Phillip and Daniel followed. Joseph went on his way to find Zebedee's stable while Daniel and Phillip left for the lower city to find the house of Jabin.

6

Zebedee's Stable

Joseph and Heber finally arrived at Zebedee's stable and found a young boy hauling water for the animals. He was a handsome boy, about ten years of age with curly hair. Joseph approached him and said. "I am Joseph of Nazareth. Your father, Zebedee, has sent me and told me you would care for my donkey."

"With due respect, sir, I am not Zebedee's son. I am his servant," answered the boy.

"Do you not have a family?"

"Oh yes, I do. They are shepherds and live near Bethlehem close to the shepherds' field."

"What are you doing here?"

"My Father owes Zebedee money. My older brothers must stay and help father with the village sheep, so I must come and work until the debt is paid."

"How long have you been here?" asked Joseph.

"I have been here almost a year."

"You must miss your family."

The young boy was silent for a moment. He swallowed hard and then answered. "My mother comes to visit when she can. I do miss my family, but when I return home, they will honor me as a man for paying this debt."

Joseph smiled at the boy. "Every father would be honored to have a son like you."

The boy smiled and then looked at Heber. "Does your donkey have a name?"

"I call him Heber," answered Joseph. "And what is your name?"

"I am called Benjamin," the boy said proudly. "Names are very important, you know. If the animals don't have a name I give them one." Benjamin reached out and took Heber's lead rope from Joseph. "Come inside the stable and I will show you where we can put Heber."

Joseph followed Benjamin into the stable.

"Would you like to know the names of the animals?" asked Benjamin.

"Certainly."

"This is Lydia. Benjamin patted the neck of the large camel. "She belongs to Zebedee's cousin, Kemuel. She is tired and sore from her long journey."

"I believe I have already met the lovely Lydia," said Joseph with a smile.

Lydia gave Joseph a snort then dropped her head and nuzzled Benjamin's hair. "She loves me," he said. "Over here is Rechel and her twin lambs, Hanna and Sarah. They were born a short time ago but Hanna has been crippled since birth. When my father gave me Rechel I had planned on using her to start my own herd some day; however, I long to be back with my family, so I must sell her and the lambs to Zebedee to help pay the debt. It will be very hard to part with them."

Benjamin pointed to the back corner. "We can put Heber over here by Ahaz."

When Joseph moved to the back of the stable with Benjamin the goat lowered his horns and glared at Joseph.

"Ahaz is a little cranky," warned Benjamin. "When he was out in the fields, he was attacked by Herod's caracal cat Felix and nearly lost his life. I've been caring for his wounds. I will make sure he is safe here."

Benjamin slipped by the grouchy goat and tied Heber to a ring in the back wall. Then he and Joseph spread fresh straw for the animals. Joseph stayed long enough to help Benjamin bring the animals their food and water.

"There will be more animals coming later, toward evening," Benjamin said. "Most of them are injured and can't work. That is why people bring them to me to watch over. They can't be left to fall prey to the wild animals that roam outside the city wall. Zebedee says I have a gift to be able to work with animals. This is a very important job, you know."

"What will Zebedee do without you when you leave?" asked Joseph.

"Oh, he will find someone. As much as I love these animals I love my family more. I want to return to my home."

Joseph placed his hand on Benjamin's shoulder "I hope you can return home soon," he said.

Joseph looked outside. "It is nearly dark outside. I must be going. I have to find my friends."

Benjamin waved good-bye to Joseph as he hurried away. Heber felt uneasy as he watched Joseph leave.

With the exception of Ahaz, the other animals in the stable seemed happy and content. Even Lydia looked peaceful. Trying to relax, Heber stretched out one hind leg, then the other and lowered his head to get some rest. No sooner had he started to doze when a loud burly soldier stormed into the stable. Heber immediately recognized him. It was the soldier Joseph had encountered earlier in the day. Balbus was bringing his horse to the stable for the night. Heber shrunk into the shadows.

"This stable needs a better cleaning. It smells in here!" Balbus shouted as he seized Benjamin by the arm.

Benjamin cried out, "Ouch! You are hurting me!"

Balbus yanked the boy close and leaned down near Benjamin's face. "I want this horse groomed and well fed," Balbus ordered. "I will return in the morning, and he will be ready; otherwise, I'll teach you the real meaning of pain. Do you understand, boy?"

Benjamin shrank back and nodded. "Yes Sir," he answered as he took the horse's reins from Balbus. "Come with me Keezhar. I'll tie you here next to Heber."

Heber did not rest well that night.

7

At The Quarry

It was early morning when Joseph came for Heber. Benjamin had just finished feeding and watering the animals. "Good morning, my friend," Joseph said to Benjamin. "Is Heber ready for our day's work?"

Benjamin smiled as he answered, "I was up before daylight and have prepared him for your arrival. I knew you would be here early."

Heber was very glad to see Joseph. Balbus had returned earlier to get Keezhar and had once again threatened the boy, Benjamin. Heber wanted to be away from the stable and near Joseph.

"I must hurry," Joseph called to Benjamin as he took Heber from the stable. "Daniel and Phillip will be waiting for me at the quarry."

By the time Joseph and Heber reached the quarry, the morning sun had already begun to heat the day. Heber was amazed at the thousands of men, some of whom were slaves, and hundreds of oxen that worked at the quarry. They moved about, taking the hewn stones from the earth.

Joseph searched the crowd of workers and found Daniel and Phillip. As Joseph approached his friends, Daniel pointed to the west side of the quarry. "There is Zebedee," he said.

Heber looked across the quarry to where Daniel had pointed. There stood Zebedee, nose to nose with the Roman centurion, Balbus. More soldiers stood nearby. Balbus began shouting angrily, but Zebedee just shrugged his shoulders and shook his head as if he did not know what the Roman was talking about. As Zebedee stepped away from the Roman, Balbus reached out and grabbed Zebedee by the arm. Zebedee jerked away. Balbus shook his fist in the face of Zebedee and the Roman moved on with the other soldiers following closely behind. Balbus pushed and shoved his way through the crowds of workers.

"They are coming this way." Phillip cried. "What should we do?"

"Help me with these panniers," ordered Joseph. The three young men turned their backs and busied themselves with the packs on Heber's back.

Once the Romans were gone, Joseph and his friends made their way through the workers to Zebedee.

"What was that about?" asked Phillip.

"The Romans are searching for anyone who might be conspiring against King Herod and the Emperor Caesar," explained Zebedee. "These Roman games have stirred up much contention among the Jewish people. Their hatred toward Herod and Caesar has increased. A man was caught when he tried to run a dagger through Caesar's heart. The Romans are concerned others might be plotting another attack against the Emperor."

"Why did they come to you?" questioned Daniel.

"As you can see, I have many men working at this site. I hear most of what is said here. If I hear talk of any conspiracy against the emperor I am to report to Herod immediately. Several of the men have been beaten and taken to the Antonia Fortress to be questioned. Already, I do not have enough men to meet Herod's demands for building his retaining wall. I cannot afford to lose any more men," Zebedee said. "But enough time wasted talking. Come with me, and I will show you where to start your day's work."

The men followed Zebedee further into the quarry. "Quarrying is a difficult and dangerous labor," Zebedee warned. "I have lost many good men to this place." He pointed to the large stones that were being loaded onto the rollers. "Some of these ashlars weigh several tons. If they are not handled properly they can crush not only men, but also the oxen that haul them. Do you still want this job?"

The men looked at each other and then nodded in agreement. "We have worked with rock before but none as large as these," said Joseph. "However, we are not strangers to hard work, and we learn quickly."

"You can go with Jabin," said Zebedee, pointing to a leathery old man approaching them. "He will teach you about the quarry."

Jabin motioned for them to follow him. He took them to several dozen men who were working to free a huge rock from the mountainside. "These rocks can be made to split along fissure lines if we can put constant pressure on them," explained Jabin. "Small holes have been drilled about three fingers apart in a straight line. We take advantage of the cracks and fissures wherever possible. The men have cut as much as they can. Wooden wedges have been driven into the cracks and soaked all night. Expansion of the wood has created enough pressure to help break the last side of the stone free." Jabin handed the men a large iron bar. "This final side will be the most difficult. I need you to help free this hewn stone from the mountain so we can load it onto the rollers."

Joseph left Heber standing close by then took his place with the rest of the men. Without hesitation, everyone tugged on the iron bars that were wedged into the last side of the rock. The men cheered as they heard the rock crack and break loose. It took 50 men working side by side to manipulate the square cut stone onto the rollers. Heavy ropes were then attached to the ashlar, and eight oxen were hitched to some of the ropes. The men used the remaining ropes to help pull. Joseph came for Heber as soon as the men and oxen began their climb up the steep slope toward the temple mount. It was a slow process. When one log rolled out from beneath the ashlar, it was picked up by the slaves and carried to the front. Extra care was taken as they placed it beneath the front of the stone. If the oxen pulled too fast the workers could be crushed by the rock. Others, with their ropes tied to the ashlar, worked to keep the rock in place. Men and oxen suffered greatly under the fierce heat of the day. They were almost to the top of the hill when one of the oxen collapsed. The heavy load started to roll slowly backward. The men, grunting and gasping, tightened the ropes to keep the hewn stone steady. Heber could see that the men and oxen were in

42

In Search of the King

trouble. Zebedee immediately ran to the lead ox and cracked his whip. "Pull, Eli! Pull!" he commanded.

A large, muscled red ox struggled to hold the team. The rocky ground was poor footing for the oxen. Slipping and sliding, oxen and men fought to keep moving upward. Other men from the quarry rushed to help steady the rock. It looked as though they were going to make it to the top, when suddenly Eli's yoke cracked and split into pieces. The remaining oxen could not hold the heavy stone. The ashlar once again rolled backward, this time dragging men and oxen.

"Cut loose! Cut loose!" ordered Zebedee. In the desperate struggle to cut the oxen free, Zebedee was knocked down. Oxen groaned as they were pulled backward and dragged down the slope. Joseph quickly grabbed his carpenter axe from Heber's panniers. He rushed toward the large ashlar and chopped frantically against the ropes that were holding the oxen. Once the oxen were loose, the men let go of the ropes and the ashlar slid down the hill. When the last roller rolled from underneath, the stone slammed to a stop at the bottom of the hill.

Phillip and Daniel ran to help the injured men. Joseph helped Zebedee to his feet. They rushed to check the teams of oxen resting near the top. Pointing to the large red ox, Zebedee told Joseph, "This is my lead ox, Eli. He is the best one I own. He will continue to pull long after the younger ones have given up." Zebedee stooped over and picked up the broken yoke. "If his yoke had held together a few minutes longer, he would have gotten us to the top. I will need a new yoke by tomorrow. This team of oxen will not work without Eli."

Joseph took the broken pieces from Zebedee. "I am a carpenter," he said. "I can have you a new one made by morning."

"It must be made of strong, hard wood. I cannot have this happen again. We have lost a day's work."

"I will have the yoke ready by morning, and it will be strong," assured Joseph. "I must hurry to the marketplace. There, I can get the supplies I need."

When Joseph and Heber reached the marketplace Joseph was directed to a man at the lower end of the city that sold the finest wood. There, Joseph found just the piece of wood he thought would make the strongest yoke and loaded it into the panniers on Heber's back. As they were leaving the market place Heber heard the sound of trumpets in the distance. He knew exactly what that meant. Caesar was here and the Roman games would begin.

8

Yonah's Survival

Felix lay near Herod's feet as Herod and Caesar watched the games. For the past several days, he had come with Herod to witness the contests, the races, and the battles. Spectators, cramped and sweltering in their seats, cheered as slaves and gladiators fought for their lives. The winners, those who survived, each approached Caesar to receive their prize.

Finally, Felix heard the call for the caracal cats. He quivered with excitement.

Herod sat his cup down and rose from his seat. Turning to Caesar, he said, "This event is one I have added for my own pleasure. I'm sure it will be one you will enjoy." Herod pointed at Felix. "You might want to wager your money on this cat."

Caesar lifted his wine cup and held it at eye level for a moment, smiling at Herod.

Herod bowed. "I must excuse myself for a moment. Felix followed proudly beside Herod as they walked toward the arena.

Herod handed Felix to his trainer then returned to his seat next to Caesar.

The trainer led Felix into the arena to compete in the event of beast against bird. As Felix passed by the seven cats from other countries, he bore his teeth and hissed, warning his opponents to stay out of his way. Felix wanted them to know that he intended to win.

As the eight cats assumed their positions around the ring, the crowd fell silent. Hundreds of caged doves were placed in the center of the ring. In the position next to Felix was a caracal from Egypt. His neck was thick and powerful. His body was long and muscled. Felix knew that many wagers had been made on which cat would knock down and kill the most doves in one fatal attack. He suspected that the cat from Egypt might be his toughest competitor. Upon a signal from the trumpeters, the owners unleashed their cats. Next the doves would be set free and the match would begin. Watching the birds in the cage, the cats crouched in anticipation, ready to spring.

In Search of the King

As the cage door opened, the crowd rose. Many leaned over the balcony to get a better view. For a moment, the confused birds huddled together until panic finally overtook a small gray dove and he flung himself heavenward. With startling swiftness the cats pounced, and the beating of wings was heard throughout the arena. Many doves hardly had a chance to leave the ground before being crushed. Others tried valiantly to get away, but in vain. With little effort, Felix sprang high into the air. Agile and accurate in his timing, he brought down one fragile bird after another. As the doves made one last effort to escape, the Egyptian cat leaping and twisting in the air, pulled several more doves to the ground.

The crowd roared in approval. Nearly every dove had been brought down, but somehow in the frenzy of the attack, Felix noticed a white dove trying to take flight at the edge of the commotion. The bird's wings beat furiously as he attempted to escape the ring, and just as Felix reached him, the white dove took flight. Confident in his ability, and just when the bird seemed out of reach, Felix leaped high above the other contenders, and with an outstretched claw, he hooked the dove, pulled him toward the ground, and pounced.

There was a flurry of feathers, but just when it seemed certain the contest was over, Felix felt the white dove slip from his grip. Suddenly there was the flapping of wings above his head. Felix leaped again, but the bird was out of reach. The white dove had escaped!

For a brief moment, Felix felt stunned. He stood there staring upward. In his mouth was a solitary white tail feather.

The crowd fell silent as the small dove flew upward and away. Suddenly, a spectator cried, "The dove is free! The dove is free!" Then everyone began pointing and cheering.

As Felix looked into the sky he saw the white dove circle above the arena and soar toward the temple mount. He was furious the dove had escaped him. He spun around to claim his remaining prey. Nearby on the ground, another dove made a feeble attempt to escape, but with one wing dragging on the ground, he could only flutter in circles. Both Felix and the Egyptian cat made a wild scramble to claim the injured bird. They reached him at the same time and at once, the two cats slammed their forepaws down onto the dove, crushing him into the dirty, bloodstained sand. With a grasp of his claws, Felix pulled the now-dead bird from his opponent. For an instant the Egyptian cat stood frozen, ears pressed back, his emerald eyes glaring at Felix. Then, without warning, he sprang forward.

At the same instant, Felix leaped and collided with the other cat in mid air. They fell to the ground, interlocked in a snarling mass of fur and claws. Felix could hear the crowd roaring again with the new turn of events. Encouraged by the cheering, Felix bit deep into the Egyptian cat's shoulder. Blood sprang from the wound. When the Egyptian cat broke loose and started to bolt away, the crowd booed. Felix pounced, his claws ripping into his opponent's back. The Egyptian cat screamed with rage and whirled to face Felix. He lashed out with his fore paw, but Felix sprang forward, sinking his teeth into the Egyptian cat's neck as he pinned his opponent to the ground.

Felix bristled as his tail whipped from side to side. The Egyptian cat howled his defeat. Felix waited for the signal to bite through the cat's throat, but the cries from the crowd voted to let the defeated cat live and the trainer quickly clasped the leash to Felix and dragged him away.

The doves that had not been so fortunate to escape were tallied and Felix was proclaimed the winner. Felix looked up toward the balcony searching for a sign of approval from Herod. Herod pointed to Felix and then looked at Caesar and smiled. The crowd cheered as the trainer returned Felix to Herod. Herod then presented the victorious cat to Caesar who hung a gold medallion around Felix's neck.

9

In The Holy Place

Timothy, a plump little dormouse, rubbed his eyes with his fists as the music of the temple services woke him. Sitting up, he peered out from his cubbyhole into the priests' court. A wisp of fragrant smoke curled up against the blue sky. The sun cast a warm glow over the pillared cloisters of the temple. The entrance to the Holy Place, where many priests had gathered, glittered with gold.

"What is happening?" Timothy thought to himself. He listened closely to the chatter of the priests.

One priest rubbed his chin and turned toward the group. "I wonder, why does Zacharias tarry so long? We've waited all morning for him to come out and give us his instruction."

"Do you suppose we should check on him?"

"No. Our lot has not been drawn to enter the temple this day. Zacharias should not be disturbed."

Timothy knew something important must have been happening. He decided to join the priests so he could hear Zacharias' message when he came out of the temple.

The priests moved about soberly as they continued to wait.

Hours passed and Timothy became impatient for Zacharias to return. He quietly slipped by the priests and looked through the doorway into the Holy Place. He could not see Zacharias. Compelled by curiosity, he moved inside. He felt uneasy because he knew he should not be there. No one was allowed in that part of the temple except the priest whose lot had been chosen.

That's odd, thought Timothy. He could hear two voices. His fur began to tingle. He moved closer so he could hear the conversation. When he reached the altar where Zacharias was burning the incense, he clasped his hand over his mouth and fell against the wall. His whiskers quivered and his body shook. There, before Zacharias, stood an angel clothed in a white robe and encircled by a burning brightness that nearly blinded Timothy.

Suddenly, he wished he'd stayed in the outer court of the temple and waited with the priests. Afraid he might suffer some dreadful consequence for being where he didn't belong, he pressed himself close to the wall and did not move. He did not want to be seen. He listened quietly as the angel spoke. The angel delivered a powerful message to Zacharias. Zacharias would have a son who would prepare the people for the Lord's coming.

Timothy quivered with excitement as he remembered the prophecy that a king would come and save the people. He thought to himself, is it time? Is this really happening, or am I dreaming?

When the angel finished speaking, the light faded and he disappeared. Timothy's legs could scarcely hold him, but somehow he managed to make his way back to the outer court where the priests were waiting. All Timothy wanted to do was get back to his home. There he could sit and think about what had just happened.

When Zacharias reached the priests waiting outside, they marveled at his condition.

"He is very pale and looks so strange," said one of the priests.

"What could be his affliction?" asked another.

Zacharias beckoned to the other priests, but he remained speechless.

"Maybe he has seen a vision," suggested one of the older men.

A young priest responded, " That could not be. Visions and revelations stopped long ago."

Another shook his head, "Perhaps he has received a curse."

Timothy knew this was no curse.

10

Finding Help

Timothy hurried back to his nest as fast as his legs would carry him. He collapsed in a heap on the floor. When he finally came to his senses he rocked back and forth praying. He was thankful his life had been spared for he knew he had been disobedient venturing into the most Holy Place. However, he did not understand why he had been allowed to live. This was the greatest message he had ever heard and he was the only one that knew what had happened to Zacharias. Wringing his tail in his hands, he said to himself, "What shall I do? What shall I do?"

Suddenly, he jumped up and packed some pieces of bread and a few seeds and placed them in his leather scrip. Then, his eyes looked across the room. There, peeking out from underneath the cloth where he had hidden it, glowed his most prized possession, a beautiful gem—a turquoise stone he had found on the Day of Atonement in the priests' courtyard. He recalled the day that he had found it. It had come loose and dropped off the high priest's vestment. Timothy wasn't a thief, but he had always admired the high priest's beautiful breastplate. The elaborate piece of cloth was woven with golden thread and inlaid with 12 precious jewels that represented the tribes of Israel.

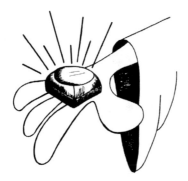

Timothy didn't think the priest would miss just one stone, so he kept the gem. It made him feel important.

He quickly tucked the gem in his scrip with the bread and seeds. He liked keeping it close.

He scurried across the courtyard to the gate that led to the outer courts of the temple. He must find someone who could tell him what he should do. After he crossed the priests' courtyard and the women's courtyard, he stopped at the gate leading into the Court of the Gentiles. He looked across the Court of the Gentiles to the huge pinnacle that stood in the southeast corner of the temple wall. It seemed so far away. Trying to shield the sun from his eyes, Timothy looked up toward the flat roof at the top of the pinnacle. "I hope he's still there," he whispered. "If he is, I know he can help me. He will know what to do."

Timothy knew in order to reach the temple wall pinnacle he had to leave the safety of the temple courts. He would have to cross the Court of the Gentiles and get inside the room where he could find the stairs that led up to the roof of the pinnacle. Crossing the Court of the Gentiles was the most dangerous part of the journey. This court was open to all. There could be Romans out there. The barbaric Romans considered fat dormice a delicacy. If they caught him, they would skin him, fry him in butter, and eat him. Timothy shuddered at that very thought. That is why he stayed in the inner courts of the temple mount where only Jews were allowed. The Jews would never consider eating a dormouse.

Timothy looked over toward the Antonia Fortress that towered next to the temple. The Roman soldiers, dressed in their red uniforms, stood out against the dismal gray building. There were no Romans in the Court of the Gentiles now, but they could come down the stairway from the fortress at any time. Even if he did make it across the Court of the Gentiles without getting caught, he wasn't sure a little dormouse like himself could make the long journey up the steep stairway. The roof of this pinnacle was the highest point on the temple mount. It would be a most difficult task. He grew tired just thinking about it. Wiping the sweat from his forehead, he slumped to the floor and leaned against the wall.

Moments later he looked out into the courtyard again. There were no red uniforms in sight. If he was going to go he must go now. He scurried as fast as he could to a large pillar and hid in its shadow. Many people were moving about and he did not want to get stepped on. After he caught his breath he hurried to another pillar, and another, until he made it across the Court of the Gentiles. Finally, when he reached the bottom of the stairway that led to the roof of the pinnacle, he gazed upward at the great flight of steps. "How will I ever make it?" he wondered.

Timothy stepped back and drew a long breath before he began the tedious climb to the top. Up and up…it seemed the stairs went on for eternity. Timothy wiped the sweat from his brow and continued. It was late afternoon before he finally reached the large flat roof of the pinnacle. Timothy took one last step and collapsed. Exhausted, he lay there for a moment. Then, staggering to his feet, he called out frantically: "Hello! Hello! Is anyone up here?"

From the far corner of the pinnacle roof came a reply. "Hello! Who are you and what do you want?"

"I'm Timothy, a temple mouse. I thought maybe you could help me."

"What makes you think I can help you?"

"Everyone knows you as Yonah, the dove who escaped Herod's cat Felix. Day after day you sit on this pinnacle and watch over Jerusalem. You see everything. Everyone says you are wise. Please, help me."

"I am here mourning the loss of my family and friends. I don't see how I can be of any help to you."

Timothy clasped his hands behind his back and hung his head. "I'm sorry," he said. "I don't mean to disturb you while you are in mourning, but this is very important."

"What could be so important that you have left the safety of the priests' courtyard and climbed up here to ask for my help?" inquired the dove.

Timothy humbly approached the dove. Suddenly he felt very nervous. His body began to shake again, and when he tried to speak the words got tangled in his mouth. "Zacharias s...s...saw—no—we s...s...saw an a...a..."

Yonah fanned Timothy with his wing. "It is hot out here and you are very excited. Maybe you should sit and rest for a moment."

Timothy felt he had no time to rest. He took a deep breath and quickly began again. "The priest, Zacharias, saw an angel and received a revelation this day in the Holy Place." There, he'd said it.

Yonah tilted his head and, squinting one eye at Timothy, he stepped backward. "How can that be?" he said. "Revelations and visits from angels stopped long ago."

"I saw the angel myself!" exclaimed Timothy.

"You saw an angel?" questioned Yonah. "Perhaps you have been in the sun too long."

"No! No! It is true. I know I saw an angel, an angel who called himself Gabriel. The angel told Zacharias that his wife, Elisabeth, will bear a son who will prepare the way for the promised Messiah, the new King who will save His people."

Yonah looked sternly at Timothy. "Do you realize what you are saying?"

"Please," Timothy pleaded. "I am telling the truth!"

Yonah hesitated for a moment before he spoke. "I do believe the temple is where we can receive heavenly instruction. I find this pinnacle to be a place of peace and comfort...but angels in the temple?"

"The temple has always been known to God's chosen people as the House of the Lord," said Timothy. "Everyone knows it is a place to receive spiritual direction."

Yonah sighed. "Unfortunately, when Herod is finished with it, it will be known as Herod's Temple. I fear there will come a day when the true meaning of the temple ceremonies will no longer exist."

"The Lord's work will always go on. The ceremonies will continue," Timothy insisted.

"Not in Herod's Temple. Besides, what good are ceremonies if the Lord ceases to dwell in a place that is not His?"

"You have escaped Herod's evil doings. You have gained great wisdom sitting up here watching all the comings and goings of this city. To all in Jerusalem you are a symbol of purity and truth. Why do you not believe me? You must study this out in your mind so you will know I speak the truth. "

Yonah looked out across the vastness of the city. "I have dreamed of the day the prophets have spoken of, the day the Messiah would come to relieve us of our burdens. A day when there would be no more animal sacrifices. Can this really be so? Oh, if I could have the wish of my heart, I would wish the words you speak to be the truth."

Timothy was determined to convince Yonah he was telling the truth. "When Zacharias questioned the angel he was given a sign. He will not be able to speak until the day that the angel's promises are fulfilled. Find Zacharias and see for yourself." Timothy insisted.

Yonah turned his attention back to Timothy. "Perhaps we should not delve into the mysteries of God. Perhaps we should not trifle with sacred things. But maybe I want to believe you. Because of your determination to convince me of these things, I will go. I will know for myself if what you say is true." Yonah spread his beautiful white wings and glided off of the pinnacle.

11

The Horror of the Night

Timothy was now alone on the top of the pinnacle. It was quiet and night was closing in around him. The noise from the activity on the temple mount had died. Only a slight trail of smoke drifted from the altar. Suddenly, he realized all the gates to the temple mount would be closed as soon as the sun cast it's last ray of light. There would not be enough time to climb back down the stairs and reach his home before he was locked out for the night. A feeling of terror crept over him. His heart pounded wildly. Looking down, Timothy tried to choke back the fear as he watched the priests shut the large gate. Now for certain he would have to spend the night on the pinnacle alone. There would be no warm nest to curl up in during the night.

Timothy slumped down and sat on the cold stone roof. Reaching into his scrip he pulled out a crumb of bread and began to nibble on it. It was dark now. He huddled in a corner as a cold night breeze swept across the top of the pinnacle. He shivered as the night grew blacker and blacker. From the pinnacle he could hear everything. "There is something creepy about the night sounds out here," he whimpered to himself. He longed to be warm and safe at home.

Closing his eyes, Timothy tried not to think about what dangers could be lurking in the darkness. Instead, he imagined himself back at the temple sanctuary where he could hear the quiet humming of the temple guards and enjoy the lingering smell of incense. With those thoughts he slipped into a quiet slumber.

Suddenly, he awoke, his eyes wide open. He thought he heard something in the valley down below the pinnacle. He was terrified that if he looked down from the pinnacle into the valley he might see something horrible. He squeezed himself closer into his corner. A chill shot through his body, and he waited. When the only sound he could hear was his own nervous breathing, he stood up and peered over the edge of the pinnacle into the darkness.

What he saw was far more frightening than he had imagined. The moon cast a dim light where Timothy could see the unmistakable shadow of a large cat slinking along the path leading to the temple. He was sure it was Herod's cat Felix. Only a short distance away, a smaller shadow, another mouse perhaps, crept along, unsuspecting of the caracal cat. Timothy knew in an instant he must do something. He pushed a loose piece of stone over the edge of the temple pinnacle. There was a moment's silence, and then came a popping sound as the stone hit the ground and broke into pieces. The smaller shadow darted out of sight.

Timothy stood frozen near the edge of the pinnacle. Far below, a pair of unblinking yellow eyes glared up at him through the darkness, then disappeared. Trembling, Timothy crouched back down in the corner. Had the cat seen him? The hair on the back of his neck tingled as he waited. Suddenly, Timothy could hear the sound of claws scraping against the wall of the pinnacle. Time dragged on. More scraping.

Timothy did not want to fall asleep, but he was so exhausted he could hardly stay awake. If only the scraping below would stop!

After what seemed an eternity, the eastern horizon began to glow and the scraping from below ceased and he began to doze. Suddenly Timothy heard the sound of padded feet moving slowly up the stairway.

12

Yonah Returns

There was nowhere to run and nowhere to hide. A large, dark shadow moved toward him and stopped a few feet away. Shaking violently, Timothy closed his eyes and waited for the cat to attack. When nothing happened he cracked one eye open. There on the roof of the pinnacle, standing a few feet away from Timothy was a priest looking for the first glow of sunlight to peek over the horizon.

A wave of relief washed over Timothy. The priest didn't even seem to notice him cowering in the corner. When the first glimmer of light appeared, the priest blew the trumpet to signal the beginning of the daily ceremonies, and then descended once again.

Alone once again, Timothy stood up and rubbed his back. He ached from sleeping on the cold, hard roof of the temple mount pinnacle. The first thing he wanted to do was to get down and find something to eat. He was starving, and his throat was sore and dry from lack of water. He looked down onto the courts of the temple. All the gates were open and the early-morning crowds were arriving. The money-changers and the animal sellers had already set up their booths in the Court of the Gentiles.

"Oh no, I'm doomed!" Timothy cried as he watched a troop of Romans enter the Court of the Gentiles. "If they stay long I will never survive up here," he sobbed. "I'm thirsty. It's too hot here, and I don't have a drop of water. I could never make it across the Court of the Gentiles with all those Romans patrolling. I will die here alone on the pinnacle! They will find nothing but a shriveled piece of fur at the end of the day."

With this final resolution, Timothy collapsed on the roof. He closed his eyes and bravely tried to endure his fate. After a while longer, he heard the glorious sound of wings. He opened his eyes. It was Yonah. He fluttered down from the sky and landed next to Timothy.

"Timothy, I have come bringing glad tidings!" announced Yonah. "I found Zacharias and it is just as you said. I should have never questioned you. We need to share this news with others."

"Yeth, yeth, we muth," replied Timothy with a swollen tongue.

"What's wrong with you?" asked Yonah.

"I'm tho hot and thirthty, I'm dying," replied the forlorn dormouse.

"Bless your frail soul. You do look a bit faint. Wait a moment. I will be back soon." Yonah took to the air, leaving Timothy alone on the pinnacle again.

"No, don't leave me here! Come back. Come back!" Timothy cried.

It felt like hours had passed and Yonah still had not returned. Just when Timothy thought he could not hang on a minute longer, Yonah appeared, clutching some pomegranate seeds. "This should help," Yonah said. "They will give you strength and quench your thirst." Timothy quickly devoured the juicy seeds. Yonah left again and returned with more seeds. "Oh, thank you," Timothy sighed. "You have saved my life!"

"Now that you have your strength back we can go and share this news. I feel that we should start by telling the animals at Zebedee's stable," said Yonah.

"We?" asked Timothy as he peered over the edge of the pinnacle. "I can't go. Don't you see all those Romans down there?"

"We can leave this evening after the Romans are gone and before they close the temple gates."

"Oh no, I can't!" Timothy said as he wrung his tail between his hands.

"Why not?"

"That means we would be outside the gates of the temple after dark. I can't go outside the temple walls at night." answered Timothy.

"What are you talking about?"

"Felix prowls around the temple at night. I would rather perish here on the pinnacle than be his next meal."

Yonah looked sternly at Timothy. "You can go, and you must."

13

Have Faith

Yonah waited with Timothy all day for the Roman soldiers to leave the temple mount. Finally, during the last hour of daylight, all the soldiers left the temple mount and returned to the Antonia fortress.

"Timothy," Yonah said, "We can go to the stable now and tell the others the news."

Timothy picked up his scrip and moved toward the stairway. "I am going straight home to the priests' court. It will be dark soon, and I've already told you I can't leave the temple mount after dark. Felix will be out there somewhere. We can leave for the stable first thing tomorrow morning."

Yonah stepped in front of him. "You came here and asked for my help. Now I am asking for yours. Tomorrow will be too late. Most of the animals at the stable will be back on the slopes of Jerusalem by dawn, grazing or working in the fields. We need to get this message to them tonight so they will be able to share it with others tomorrow."

"Why can't you go and tell them?"

"You are the only one who saw the angel. You need to tell them."

Timothy shook his head. "No! No! No! It is too dangerous out there!"

Yonah tried to comfort Timothy. "I see you are afraid," he said. "But let us go about this task with faith, not fear. I believe the Lord will protect us from harm."

"That's easy for you to say when you're up there and I'm down here. Can't we wait and let the Lord protect us in the daylight when Felix is at Herod's palace. We are no match for that beast."

Yonah continued to council Timothy. "You must find the courage to leave the safety of the temple and come with me to testify of what you have seen. God will protect us."

Timothy slumped down. He pressed his hands together and rocked back and forth.

"What manner of mouse are you, Timothy?" Yonah asked. "You must have more faith."

Timothy's voice quivered as he spoke, "I'm a scared mouse, and maybe a dead mouse, but I will go."

Timothy slowly climbed down the stairway. Only a few people lingered in the Court of the Gentiles. The marble colonnades cast long, eerie shadows across the courtyard. Timothy's rapid tiptoe between the shadows kept him from being exposed in the open for any length of time. Even though Timothy's insides churned in terror, he took a deep breath and tried to suppress his fear. He reached inside his scrip and touched his stone. Maybe it would help him have the courage he needed to do this task.

When he reached the east gate, he looked out into the coming night. A peculiar horror seemed to accompany the approaching darkness. The whiskers on Timothy's nose began to quiver. He twisted his tail between his hands until it was all crunched up. Cautiously he stepped outside the gate, but quickly scurried back in again. To step from the safety of the temple walls into the night almost certainly meant death in the most gruesome manner. He did not want to be eaten. Several more times he stepped across the threshold of the gate, then back again. Finally, Yonah, who was circling above, flew down and landed. "What are you doing?" he asked.

"I like the feeling I get when I am inside the temple walls but I don't like the feeling I get when I am outside the temple walls."

"Don't worry, Timothy, I am flying high where I can see everything. I can warn you of any approaching dangers. Remember, salvation comes to those who are willing to sacrifice for the Lord's work," reassured Yonah.

"But I don't want to sacrifice my life," whimpered Timothy. "I'm not ready to die. I especially don't want to be eaten by Felix."

"Timothy you must make up your mind. The priests will be here any moment to shut the gate."

Timothy knew that once the gate was shut he could not get back in until morning. But he knew what must be done. Again he reached inside his scrip to touch his precious gem. It was as though it could give him the power to leave the temple mount. He closed his eyes as he took his final step outside the temple walls. Opening his eyes, he looked up to make sure Yonah was with him. Then, stealing from rock to bush, he scurried toward the stable while Yonah soared above leading the way.

The pair had not gone far when Timothy thought he saw a familiar shadow. He stopped to get a closer look, but the shadow disappeared. Timothy looked toward the sky to make sure Yonah was still with him. The dove was there and did not seem alarmed so Timothy decided to continue on. Once again the shadow appeared directly in front of him. Timothy froze.

"Boo!" barked a large, hairy beast as he jumped toward Timothy.

Timothy collapsed on the ground and everything went black. When he awoke, he staggered to his feet, dizzy-eyed, looking for a place to hide. Then he heard Yonah's voice.

"Why did you do that, Baruch?" asked the dove.

Instead of a ferocious cat, Timothy saw a mangy dog standing before him..

Timothy took a deep breath and tried to speak but no words came out.

"What's the matter, cat got your tongue?" Baruch laughed.

Yonah continued scolding the dog, "That was not funny. Now see what you've done?"

"Ah, I didn't hurt him," Baruch said. "He will be fine."

"Stop this nonsense Baruch," warned the dove. "We are engaged in a marvelous contribution to the Lord's work and you are trying to be funny."

Suppressing a chuckle, Baruch sat down and began scratching behind his ear. "What could be so marvelous that you can't enjoy a good laugh?" he asked.

"Enjoyment should not come at the expense of others," said Yonah. He turned to Timothy. "It is all right," he comforted. "It is only Baruch. He is harmless."

"Harmless?" Baruch puffed out his chest and pranced around. "I'll have you know I am not harmless. I am a fearless."

"I did not mean to insult you," Yonah apologized. "I just meant to say that you would not hurt Timothy or me. We are safe in your presence."

"I accept the apology and now may I ask what is this marvelous work you spoke of?" questioned Baruch.

"If you would escort us to Zebedee's stable so we can deliver a divine message to the animals there, you will discover this marvelous work that is about to come forth."

"I don't have anything better to do," sighed Baruch. "I might as well see you safely to your destination."

"That would be greatly appreciated," said Yonah. "But if I detect the slightest hint of mischief, you will have to be excused. Promise me, no more practical jokes."

"For you Yonah, I will try really hard to be good," Baruch promised.

Yonah looked at Timothy. "Just stay close to Baruch and he will make sure you reach the stable safely."

Timothy, still trembling, was relieved that Yonah had provided him with his own personal bodyguard; however, he maintained a healthy dose of skepticism toward his assigned protector.

14

An Important Message

Heber rested in the stable after a long days work at the quarry. The other animals were also settling down for the night. Suddenly, a white dove flew into the stable and landed on a ledge. Right behind him through the door followed a dog and a plump little dormouse. Heber recognized the dog as the one from the marketplace who had defended the beggar. He had never seen such a mouse before and wondered how this odd trio came to be together.

Ahaz, the cranky goat was the first to question the intentions of the threesome. He looked at the dove and then at Timothy. "How could you lower yourselves to keep company with this worthless, disgusting scavenger? Don't you know dogs cannot be trusted? He keeps company with all the beggars who loiter around the marketplace, looking for handouts."

Baruch scratched his belly. "It must be a defect in my character. I like to eat."

Ahaz dropped his head and aimed his horns toward Baruch. "What do you think you are doing here anyway?"

"I just thought I would stop by to cheer you up," answered Baruch.

"We have no handouts today," bleated Ahaz. "Go back to where you came from. We do not keep company with your kind. You are nothing but a scabby mongrel." Ahaz deliberately advanced toward Baruch. "You are not welcome here."

The grayish-brown hair stood up in a ridge on Baruch's back and a low growl warned the goat to keep his distance. "Listen here Big Billy, I'm staying," Baruch said.

The furious goat put his head down and charged toward Baruch. "The name is Ahaz and no, you are not staying," he bellowed.

In Search of the King

Yonah quickly flew down and landed in front of Ahaz. "Stop!" he ordered. "We have come bearing glad tidings. The important message we are here to deliver is for everyone. Baruch is welcome here."

"What message is that?" questioned Ahaz suspiciously.

"The day for which Israel has waited and prayed is about to come forth," said Yonah.

"What are you talking about?" asked the ox, Eli.

Timothy quietly scurried up to the rim of a manger. In his strongest voice he announced, "A new king will soon be born that will save his people!"

Murmurs of astonishment spread throughout the stable.

Ahaz looked Timothy in the eye. "You are a frumpy little mouse. Sounds like you've been dipping in the priests' wine."

"Why should we have to put up with your insults?" Baruch growled. "You have the disposition of a scorpion. Have you ever thought about improving your social skills?"

Ahaz lowered his horns, and glared at the dog.

"You are going to get a cramp in your face if you keep scowling like that," Baruch warned.

Ahaz took another step toward the dog. "I'm not one bit happy about you being here so you better hold your tongue." Baruch turned and walked away from Ahaz, "Who ever is in charge of your happiness is obviously not doing a good job," he barked.

"Please," insisted Rechel, the mother ewe. "This is no time to argue. I don't believe this mouse has been dipping in the priests' wine! We need to listen to what he has to say."

The animals in the stable quieted.

Yonah flew up to the top of a manger. "Tell them, Timothy," he said. "Tell them what happened in the temple."

Timothy hesitated for a moment. He wanted to remember every detail of his experience. "The priest, Zacharias, was visited by an angel of the Lord while he was burning incense in the temple. The angel, who called himself Gabriel, told Zacharias that his wife, Elisabeth would bear a son who would prepare the way for our king, the promised Messiah."

"That can't be," argued Ahaz. "Angels, visions, and revelations stopped long ago."

"Yes," agreed Eli. "I have worked many years hauling ashlars to help build Herod's temple, and I have never heard about any visions or revelations."

"Why do doubts arise in your heart?" questioned Yonah. "The temple is where the mysteries of God can be revealed. With God, nothing is impossible."

"How can we know what you say is the truth?" questioned Ahaz suspiciously.

"I have found out for myself," said Yonah, "but if you'll remember the words of the prophet Isaiah and search your heart, you too can know."

"Oh, I love the words of Isaiah," sighed Lydia. Her long eyelashes fluttered. "They bring gladness to my heart."

Yonah continued. "Isaiah said the Messiah would be preceded by a special messenger. His words have given us a prophetic glimpse of the future."

"You bird brain," neighed the Roman stallion, Keezhar. "No one can see into the future."

Eli took a step toward Keezhar. "Bridle your tongue," he ordered.

"Isaiah says that this King will free His people. He will be of royal blood, a descendant of King David and will be born of a virgin," said Yonah.

"Oh, I love the words of Isaiah," repeated Lydia.

"Isaiah, Isaiah, I-say-ah you're all crazy. There are no such things as angels and signs and prophets who can see into the future," insisted Keezhar.

"The words we speak are true," testified Timothy. "I saw an angel. I believe God will help us."

Keezhar snorted. "What has your God done for you, except to lead you into captivity?"

"Our God is sending us a new king, to free us from this Roman bondage," replied Rechel.

"When is He coming?" asked Sarah, one of the twin lambs.

"I hope soon," their mother answered.

"The prophets say there will be signs preceding the birth of the king," said Yonah, "many of which have already come to pass."

"Signs?" sneered Keezhar. "Show me a sign."

"Here is your sign," Lydia walked over and smacked Keezhar with her hip. "Take that, you pompous horse."

"That's no sign," snorted Keezhar.

"Please," begged Rechel. "This should be a time of joy and peace. What a magnificent promise the birth of this child holds for us. We will have a new king."

"You already have a king," interrupted Keezhar. "Herod is your king."

Lydia spit. "A sorry king old Herod is. He's a disgrace to the whole Jewish nation."

"The Romans rule this world, and as long as they do, Herod will be your king," said Keezhar.

15

A Humble Servant

Heber had been silently absorbing the wonderful words spoken by Timothy and Yonah, their talk of a new king. He whispered to himself, "Oh, how wonderful it would be to serve such a king."

"What did you say?" asked Timothy.

"Oh," said Heber, "it wasn't important."

"Please share your thoughts with us," said Rechel.

Heber hesitated for a second. "I just thought it would be a real honor to serve such a king as the promised Messiah."

Keezhar's wild laughter echoed through the stable. "You? Serve a king?" Again he laughed long and loud. "Look at you. You're a lowly donkey. What kind of a king would want you?"

Heber shrank back into the shadows of the stable.

Keezhar towered over Heber "The privilege of serving a king would be reserved for one of my stature," he said. "You're so... small. Look at your long, dangling ears and your coarse hair. My soft white coat is meticulously groomed."

"Almost white coat," corrected Baruch. "Dirty gray is more like it."

Keezhar ignored him and continued. "My ears are refined. And look at my noble head," he turned his head slightly. "It's perfect. Your head is too big. And that nose...I've never seen a nose quite like that in all of Rome. And do you call that a tail? When I parade down the streets, people notice."

Lydia leaned down and whispered in Baruch's ear, "Someone ought to poison his oats."

Baruch nodded his head in agreement.

In Search of the King

Keezhar rambled on. "My legs are graceful and I move with ease. Your legs are short and you shuffle when you walk. That wheezing noise you make when you talk...ah, well, what can I say? You're nothing but an ugly beast of burden, unfit for a king."

Heber's ears went down and his head hung lower and lower. A tear trickled down his long nose. He wished he had kept silent. He could have avoided the humiliation.

"Since Herod was appointed the ruler over the Jewish people," interrupted Eli, "we've all become beasts of burden."

Rechel tried to comfort Heber. "Don't listen to Keezhar," she said. "He's just bitter because his coat wasn't quite white enough, so he wasn't selected to dwell in the royal stables."

Keezhar snorted.

Ahaz approached Keezhar. "Where did you acquire such vast amounts of pride, you stiff-necked, sway-bellied nag?" he said. "No one is so great that he has the right to criticize another. It is far better to know your own weaknesses and imperfections than to point out those of others. You need to tame your ego."

Baruch rolled his eyes heavenward.

Keezhar laid back his ears and charged toward Ahaz. "Why, you crusty old goat!"

Lydia stepped in front of Keezhar to stop the attack and Keezhar slid to a stop to avoid a collision with her.

"Where do you think you are going?" she asked.

Yonah flew down from the ledge and landed on the manger next to Heber. "God is no respecter of persons. While Keezhar looks on the outside, God looks on the heart. You don't have to be the biggest, the best, the most talented, or the most beautiful to serve, only the most willing. Remember, it is His most humble servants whom God chooses to do His greatest work."

Heber lifted his head as he listened to Yonah's council. "You, Heber, stand for humility and as a token of peace," said Yonah. "Isaiah says that our King will be called the Prince of Peace. I believe it would be just fine for you to serve such a king."

"Oh, I love the words of Isaiah," Lydia sighed again.

"Yes," stated Eli. "If it weren't for his words, we might not understand these mysteries."

"We need to listen to the prophecies of Isaiah," said Rechel. "This is our day to prepare for the coming of a new king. We can all serve Him."

Shaking his head and stamping his foot, Keezhar yelled, "Quiet! I will not allow any more of this nonsense."

Lydia looked at Baruch. "Who made him the ruler over this stable?" she snorted.

Baruch shrugged his shoulders. "He didn't get my vote."

"I'm the boss of this stable and I will hear no more talk of a new king!" demanded Keezhar. "Herod is your king.

Fluttering her eyelashes at Keezhar, Lydia stuck her nose in his face. "You are not our boss. Remember your ill breeding has caused you to be here with us instead of at the palace's royal stable with the prized chariot horses. You owe Herod no honors. Your continued loyalty to the wicked king Herod will bring you no reward."

Suddenly a faint ray of sunlight shone through the stable entrance, Heber realized they had spent all night discussing the promise of the new king and wondering—when was he coming?

16

Balbus Strikes Again

S everal days had passed since Yonah, Baruch and Timothy had visited the stable but Heber could not stop thinking about the wonderful message they had brought. He thought maybe if there were a new king that ruled over Jerusalem, life wouldn't be so hard.

By the time Joseph arrived to get Heber that morning, the sun was already shining through the door of the stable. Heber knew it would be another long day at the quarry and he was not looking forward to being there. Every morning when Joseph had come for Heber, Benjamin had him ready and waiting.

Heber lifted his weary head and pricked up his ears as Joseph walked through the stable door.

"Good morning Joseph!" Benjamin called.

Benjamin gave Heber a fistful of dried grass before he handed Heber's lead rope to Joseph. "Heber is ready for the day."

"You are a good young man," Joseph said to Benjamin. "Your parents should be very proud of you." He reached out and patted the boy on the back. "I need to go to work now, but I'll visit with you when I return tonight."

When Joseph and Heber reached the quarry, Zebedee greeted them. "Joseph," he said, "you have been one of my best workers here at the quarry. You never quit until a job is finished. I hate to lose you as a worker, but you are being reassigned."

"What do you mean?" asked Joseph.

"With the men and oxen working together these past few weeks, we have been able to get many of the large hewn stones over the hill and to the temple mount. We have made great progress on the retaining wall. However, the work on the temple mount itself is not getting done as fast as Herod would like, and a man came yesterday looking for more help. He saw the yoke you made for Eli and wanted to know whose hands had made such a fine piece. You did an excellent job, Joseph. It is not only strong, but it is appealing to the eye."

"I'm glad you like it," Joseph said. "But if you are pleased with my work, then why can I not stay here and work for you?"

"I have been asked to send you to the temple mount tomorrow so your skill as a carpenter is better put to use. This will be an opportunity for you to work with some of the finest craftsmen in Herod's kingdom. You can finish up your work today at the quarry, and tomorrow you will go to work at the Temple of Herod."

This was good news to Heber. He had grown weary of climbing up and down the hills all day between the quarry and the temple mount. Perhaps with Joseph working at the temple as a carpenter, he and Joseph would not have to work so hard.

Finally, that evening, when their work at the quarry was finished, Heber and Joseph left with the other workers. Everyone moved slowly down the path toward the city.

Suddenly, Heber felt something cut across his hind legs. He lunged forward. The pain stung terribly.

"Get that donkey out of my way!" a voice cried out from behind him.

Heber looked back and was horribly afraid when he saw Keezhar and his Roman master, Balbus, towering over him. Balbus held a whip in his hand.

Balbus yelled at Joseph. "Clear the way!" He pulled the whip back to strike again. Heber braced himself for the next sting.

Immediately Joseph grabbed the end of the whip and yanked it from the Roman's hand.

Balbus dismounted and walked boldly toward Joseph. When he reached Joseph he struck him in the face. Joseph stood in rigid silence. Jaw clenched and void of emotion, he continued to face his attacker. The Roman leaned back and inflicted another powerful blow. Still there was no response from the humble carpenter. A third time, Balbus pulled back his fist and hit Joseph in the face. Joseph's head jerked backward, but he stood firm.

"You are a stubborn Jew," Balbus snapped. Determined to knock Joseph down, the Roman prepared to strike him again. But when Balbus noticed the workers gathering around with iron pry bars and mallets in hand, he dropped his fist to his side. Then he leaned over and whispered to Joseph, "I'll be back, Jew."

Heber was relieved when Balbus climbed back into the saddle, spun Keezhar around, and galloped away.

Daniel and Phillip were the first to reach Joseph. "Are you all right?" Daniel asked.

"I'll be fine," Joseph said, as he bent down and stroked the welts on Heber's back legs.

"This isn't right, Joseph," Daniel complained bitterly. "Why do we have to endure the cruelty from these Roman pigs? If Israel ruled instead of Rome, you and Mary would be the rightful heirs to the throne. The rights of the Davidic family go unrecognized. Instead we have to endure this Roman bondage with a king they have appointed."

"Herod's pretense of nobility is disgusting," said Phillip. "He does not have the right to assume a title of which he is not worthy."

Joseph placed his hand on Phillip's shoulder. "We must remember that salvation is not found in titles or worldly possessions," Joseph answered.

Just then Zebedee frantically pushed through the crowd. "Joseph, your life is in danger. You must leave Jerusalem at once. That Roman will be back. Only next time he won't be alone."

"I do not fear him. I have done nothing wrong," Joseph insisted.

"It matters not that you are innocent of wrongdoing. Jews are arrested and beaten every day on false charges." Zebedee shoved a bag full of coins into Joseph's hand. "Here is your week's pay. You must go. If they find you here they will arrest us both and throw us in prison. Go now before he returns."

Joseph looked at Zebedee. "If it puts your life in jeopardy then I will go," he said. "However, I would ask one thing of you before I leave." Joseph handed the bag of coins back to Zebedee. "Let the boy at the stable take his sheep and go home."

Zebedee looked at Joseph and paused for a moment then he nodded his head, "I will do as you ask."

Heber followed Joseph as he turned and walked toward the road that would take them back home to Nazareth.

17

Back Home

Nazareth was a welcome sight to Heber. It was good to be home. Joseph put Heber in the lean-to, then left to find Mary. Heber had just started to nap when the old rooster Ezra appeared.

"Well, Heber, you are home," Ezra said. "I thought I would stop by and warn you I think Naomi is on her way here to greet you. I saw her with the other hens trailing behind her headed this way. I'm wondering what they are hatching up now. I'm sure they will want to know all about your journey to the city."

"There is nothing to tell," Heber replied.

Just then Naomi came flitting across the courtyard. She stopped directly in front of Heber. "What happened to Joseph? she asked. "His face is black and blue."

Heber was silent.

"Didn't things go well in the Holy City?" she pried.

Heber refused to answer. Naomi droned on. "Mary just returned a week ago from visiting her cousin Elisabeth, you know." Naomi shook her head and wriggled her tail feathers. "It's ridiculous that a young girl like Mary should go flitting around the countryside. She should stay home and learn how to be a good Jewish wife so she can prepare for her marriage – unless there is not going to be a marriage. I've heard whisperings at the market that there is not going to be a wedding."

Heber whipped his tail from side to side and turned his back on Naomi.

Naomi strutted around to face him again. "Maybe Joseph can't provide for a wife. I dare say if his trip to Jerusalem was not very profitable he will not be able to pay Mary's father the dowry. But what can you expect from a simple carpenter?"

Heber was tired from the long journey home and he had finally had enough of Naomi's gossip. "I will hear no more from you!" he brayed.

Shocked by his outburst, Naomi stuttered, "Wha-wha-what did you say?"

"Let me interpret," crowed Ezra. "SHUT YOUR BEAK! Heber is not interested in your foul gossip. He has neither the time nor the interest to listen to any more of your nonsense so go strut your stuff somewhere else!"

Naomi turned to the flock and with wide eyes clucked, "I must leave this place before I'm plucked bare of the respect I deserve."

Ruffling her feathers and sticking her beak in the air, Naomi left Heber's lean-to, stomped past the old rooster, Ezra, and continued on to where the rest of the hens were waiting. When the last tail feather disappeared from view, Heber looked at Ezra. "Well done my friend. I guess you put that gossipy old hen in her place."

"After you spoke to her Heber I wasn't sure she was going to get her eye lids pulled back over her eye balls," cackled Ezra. "That's one hen that loves to talk but can't be bothered listening. It would be a welcome miracle to find a way to stop her chatter."

"Not a soul in Nazareth has escaped her tongue of mischief," said Heber "She is always stewing about something."

Speaking of stew…" Ezra paused and scratched the dirt, "I'm actually worried for the old hen. I hear she hasn't laid an egg for several months and you know what happens to hens that don't lay eggs. She could end up in the meat market sold as a stewing hen."

Heber didn't want to talk about Naomi any longer so he changed the subject. "How is your crowing voice, Ezra?" he asked.

"Oh, It's a little raspy, but I'm getting along." Ezra paraded around, showing off his feathers. "I'm really in pretty good shape for my age, you know. I still have all of my beautiful feathers."

Heber nodded in agreement. Ezra did indeed still have his feathers, but Heber was worried about what Ezra would do if he could no longer crow.

"I best be getting back to my perch next door," said Ezra. "Someone needs to keep watch on those hens. It is good to have you and Joseph back in Nazareth again, Heber."

"Thank you, Ezra. You are a good neighbor and it is good to be back in Nazareth."

It was several days before Heber saw Naomi again and when he did he was bewildered at her behavior. She came flying, jumping, and twirling in the air. When she reached Heber she exclaimed. "Oh, Heber you should have been there! It was wonderful! The moon was shinning brightly. The stars twinkled in the heavens. You should have seen the roadway all lit up with hundreds of oil lamps." Naomi twirled around. "There were people dancing and singing. Daniel and Phillip came all the way from Jerusalem to be with Joseph. It was a heavenly night in Nazareth. Mary was the most beautiful bride I have ever seen and Joseph was so handsome! It is a perfect marriage. I tell you, it is true love. Joseph will take such good care of her."

Heber stared blankly at Naomi as she flitted out of courtyard dancing whirling and jumping in the air.

PART
2

Months Later...

18

Bao News

Heber truly enjoyed his life with Mary and Joseph. Since Joseph had found plenty of work in Nazareth they had not had to travel and Heber did not have to work so hard. He didn't think life could get any better. The days were getting warmer and everyone seemed to be happy.

Even Naomi had not been around to complain or ask questions.

Heber was resting beneath the shade of the lean-to when he suddenly noticed a cloud of dust in the distance. Something was moving toward the city. At first he thought it might be another caravan bringing supplies and visitors to Nazareth, but as it drew closer he recognized the red cloaks of Roman soldiers. He shuddered as the soldiers marched with stern faces past him and straight to the public market.

Heber looked over the short stone wall that separated Joseph's yard from his neighbor's yard. There he could see Ezra watching the Romans from the rooftop. He always kept a watchful eye on the town—and his hens. After a while, he flew down and made his way over to Heber. "I wonder why we are being infested with those Romans."

"I'm not sure," replied Heber. "But it can't be good."

"I'm going to the market place to find out."

"Be careful," Heber warned as he watched the old rooster flap to the top of the wall, and disappear to the other side. "Those Romans are dangerous."

Heber felt restless as he waited for Ezra to return. He didn't have to wait long. A short time later, Ezra reappeared in the yard. "Heber," he choked, "The Romans have delivered terrible news to Nazareth!"

"What news?" Heber asked worriedly.

Ezra marched back and forth as he explained. "The captain of the Romans posted a decree that has been sent out from the Roman Emperor Caesar Augustus. Caesar is insisting that tribute by taxation must be paid to the Roman Empire. He has ordered a taxing of the people in all kingdoms and provinces in the empire." Ezra's voice became raspier as he spoke. "This Roman ruler once again has revealed his greed. As soon as our people start to prosper, Caesar orders Herod to tax them more so they do not prosper. The Roman rule is strangling the Jewish people." Ezra twisted his neck around in a dramatic attempt to convey the message.

Heber lowered his head, "It's not right."

Ezra stopped, raised his wing in the direction the Romans had come. "I wish we could send all the Romans back to Rome!"

"Ezra," said Heber, "do you believe someday a king will be born who will free his people of this Roman bondage?"

Ezra stopped and scratched his head. "I haven't really thought much about it," he said. "The rabbi in the synagogue preaches that there will be a deliverer who will reign in righteousness over the Jews. But I'm not sure it will be in our day. We are both growing old, and I'm afraid it is too late for us to be saved by a new ruler. Besides, he would have to be a very powerful king to defeat the Roman Empire."

"I guess you are right," said Heber. "Poor Joseph, he works very hard for little money and now he will have to pay even more taxes to Caesar." He shook his head.

"Heber," Ezra continued, "The worst part of this decree is that all the men are required to register at the place they claim as their ancestral home.

"But for Joseph that means traveling to Bethlehem. "

"Yes, Joseph must travel to Bethlehem, the city of David, to be counted and taxed accordingly under the imperial decree."

Heber's mind sorted through Ezra's words. "But Mary is with child. She will not stay here alone without Joseph. How can she travel in her condition? Certainly, Joseph will have to stay here with her until her baby is born."

"I think not," said Ezra, "even Joseph will not be able to escape the demands of Caesar. I fear the dreadful consequences that might be inflicted on those who ignore the decree."

19

Time to Say Good-Bye

Several days later, Heber gazed out of his shelter at the soft morning light creeping over the horizon. He had been awake much of the night thinking about the events that had taken place during the past few months. The thought of leaving Nazareth again weighed heavy on his heart. He had found joy and comfort here with Joseph and Mary. Now the Romans were forcing them to leave the safety of their home and travel across rough and difficult terrain to Bethlehem.

He remembered when he had first heard the decree, a few days earlier and how overwhelmed he had felt—even discouraged. How would Mary ever make the journey to Bethlehem? Why had God let these hardships come upon good people like Joseph and Mary? Sometimes God's mysteries tend to question the mind, he had thought to himself. Joseph must have great faith that God would watch over them and protect them. Heber did not want to leave Nazareth, but his heart told him it was the right thing to do. He would go to Bethlehem with Joseph and Mary. He would serve them wherever they traveled.

The next morning, Joseph was up early and packed Heber's panniers with all the provisions needed for the long wearisome journey that lay ahead.

Heber wondered why Ezra had not stopped by to tell him good-bye. It would be a sad occasion not to see Ezra before he left. Even Naomi had not visited recently.

Suddenly, from the neighboring yard, an unusual commotion erupted. Heber turned his head to see a merchant carrying two cages. He passed by Heber and walked toward a small brown cart at the edge of the road. In one cage, Heber saw Naomi squawking and flopping around trying to get out of the cage. In the other cage, Ezra peered longingly at Heber but could not utter a sound.

From across the yard, Heber watched as Joseph's neighbor waved his hand toward the merchant. "The hen hasn't laid an egg in nearly a year, and the rooster can't crow anymore. Sell them in the market for stew meat and pay me when you return this way."

Heber's heart sank. Poor Ezra. Alas, his beautiful tail feathers had not saved him, and even though Naomi was bothersome at times, Heber did not like seeing her caged and sold for stew meat. He watched them until they disappeared down the road. He mourned for his friends as he thought about how brutal life could be.

Within an hour, Heber, Joseph, and Mary joined the caravan that was leaving for Bethlehem.

20

The City of David

The caravan moved along during the day stopping occasionally for food and water. The spring days were warm but the nights were cold. During the second day of travel Heber noticed four men in the distance following the caravan. Sometimes they would disappear, only to reappear at some later point along the trail. Heber wondered if anyone else had seen them. What did they want? Heber thought. Why did they keep following? Heber knew it was not unusual for bandits to follow a caravan until they found a straggler to rob. He wished they would soon get to the city where they would be safe.

Finally, they were within a day's journey of Bethlehem. The early morning sun shone brightly and although Heber was tired, he was relieved they would soon be where they could rest.

The caravan was preparing to leave and Joseph reached out to help Mary onto Heber's back. He brushed a strand of hair from her face.

The traveling had become difficult for Mary. Each day it became harder for her to keep pace with the caravan. Much of the day found her sitting atop the panniers on Heber's back. The panniers were heavy, and the added weight would normally have seemed difficult, but somehow, Heber found the strength to continue. He found joy in helping Joseph care for Mary.

When the sun was high in the sky Joseph stopped to let Mary and Heber rest.

The leader of the caravan called to Joseph, "We must not stop or we will not arrive at the city in time to find lodging for the night."

"Go ahead without us, we will follow soon," Joseph replied.

"It is too dangerous to travel alone," the man warned. If you do not enter the city by nightfall, you are taking a risk whether or not you will arrive safely."

The leader of the caravan looked toward the hill where the four men had last been seen. "You could be robbed—or worse. I'm sorry we cannot wait for you. We are already short on time."

"I understand," said Joseph, "But we will rest here for a while and then continue on shortly. "

Heber watched as the caravan began moving and slowly disappeared over the next hill.

In the distance, four men appeared briefly on the horizon then vanished out of sight.

Heber felt a wave of panic well up inside of him as he suddenly realized that he, Joseph, and Mary were now alone.   He

In Search of the King

desperately wanted to be brave, but every instinct told him it would have been better to stay with the caravan.

After some time, Joseph helped Mary back onto Heber's back and the three of them moved along the stony road toward Bethlehem. Heber tried to keep pace with Joseph as they moved along, but mostly he took great care with each step. He carefully picked his way around the obstacles in his path so as not to stumble with his precious cargo. He promised himself that he would deliver Mary safely to the city, no matter how far, no matter how difficult.

Suddenly, Heber heard a rock break loose and clatter down the slope nearby. Heber turned to see the four men descending upon them. Heber felt uneasy as he watched the men move closer and closer to them, but Joseph showed no sign of fear.

The men's faces, parched from the sun were stern and weathered. The leader was a brawny fellow with a dirty tunic, thick gray hair, and a long matted beard. A dagger dangled in its case from a wide leather belt around his waist. He was also missing two fingers on his right hand, probably taken as punishment for a crime he had committed.

Joseph stood between Mary and the men who now blocked his passage.

The leader drew his dagger from its sheath and roared, "Empty your bags!"

Joseph bowed his head and quietly replied, "I will gladly give you what I have in the bags," he paused, "but I would ask you to let us pass."

One of the men stepped toward Joseph and sneered, "Why should we not kill you and take that old donkey to feed our dogs?"

Heber, not wanting Mary to sense his fear, tried not to tremble.

Joseph glanced toward Mary. "My wife is with child. Her time is near and we must reach the City of David by nightfall. Again, I ask you to let us pass."

The man looked at Joseph, then at Mary. His brow furrowed and Heber could see a troubled look in his eye. "Why should I care about either of you?" he asked Joseph.

"Because it would be honorable to do so."

The man laughed loudly, "And what of taking your possessions? Is that honorable?"

"I would consider it to be payment for your services," replied Joseph.

"What services?" the man questioned.

"We need your help. You could safely escort us the remainder of the way to the City of David, and in exchange for your protection you can keep whatever possessions you want." It would make a difference to us and it would bring honor to you."

The leader waited for a moment before speaking again. Looking at Joseph, he said, "I could kill you now and keep whatever I want anyway."

He then looked toward Mary. The man was thinking about something, but Heber couldn't tell if the robber intended to kill them or spare them. Finally, after what seemed like forever, the leader's eyes gradually softened and his countenance changed. Slowly, he slid his dagger back into its sheath. "There is something different about you," he said. "My men and I will see you safely to Bethlehem."

"Thank you," Joseph said. "May God bless you with far greater rewards than the contents in our bags."

Heber felt a surge of relief wash over him. He took a deep breath and started along the rocky path again. The going was not easy, but Heber felt blessed that they had been spared and he gladly carried Mary on his back. Heber knew that many victims had been robbed and left by the roadside to perish by men such as these. He did not understand why the robbers had allowed them to live, but he was grateful.

It was late in the day when they finally arrived at the junction just outside of the town. "This is where we leave you," the leader of the gang said. "You are safe now."

Joseph thanked the men again. "You have helped us much," he said.

As the four men turned to leave, Joseph called, "Wait! You haven't taken your payment with you."

The leader turned and waved his arm, "Not this time," he said. "This time we do it for the child. Goodbye."

Heber watched as the men walked back up the road and disappeared over the hill. Mary and Joseph watched also. A few minutes later, Mary, Joseph, and Heber started the rocky descent down the hill toward the city.

When they finally entered the small town of Bethlehem, Heber could see that many people had come in obedience to Caesar's decree. People huddled together in the streets and shared blankets to keep warm. Others were camped on the ridge above the city. Joseph led Heber down the street toward an inn. Many people were gathered around the door of the inn. Joseph found a quiet place away from the crowd for Heber and Mary to rest while he left to find the innkeeper. Heber knew Mary must be exhausted from the long journey but she never uttered a word of complaint.

Heber watched as Joseph worked his way through the crowd to the entrance of the inn where he introduced himself to the innkeeper. "I am Joseph of Nazareth. I am of the linage of David. I have come with my wife Mary to be counted of Caesar. My wife is with child and I am concerned that she is near her time. Have you a place we can stay?"

The keeper shook his head. "This door has welcomed many a traveler but there is no more room here at this inn tonight. I know of no accommodations left in all of Bethlehem."

"Please," Joseph said. "She is weary and needs somewhere to rest. We have no family here and we have nowhere else we can stay."

"I'm sorry." The man stopped and stroked his beard as he stared at the ground in thought. "Wait a moment," he said. He stepped inside the gate and called out to a young man coming across the courtyard. "Hurry, quickly."

"Yes, father. I am coming," replied the gangly youth.

"Take this man and his wife and show them the small stable just down over the hill behind the bluff. It is the one overlooking the east."

Before Joseph left he took the innkeeper's hand and vigorously shook it. "My thanks to you, sir. May God's blessing be upon you."

The young man led them through a passage paved with stone. From there they followed a dirt path that led down a slope toward the cave-like stable. When they reached the small enclosure, the youth apologized. "It's only a stable, but maybe it can offer you the privacy you need."

"We are simple people," replied Joseph. "We are grateful for your kindness."

The youth bowed to Joseph, then turned and departed. Heber was content with the stable's privacy. He watched as Joseph went about making their accommodations more comfortable. After cleaning the stable, Joseph brought in some new straw. Heber savored the smell of the freshly spread straw. He was grateful to finally retire after a long day's journey. Joseph furnished Mary with her own little corner of the stable away from everything else.

Then he helped her brush the oats from the bottom of one of the mangers and he filled it with the clean straw. Mary would now have a place to put her baby that would soon be born.

21

The Shepherds' Field

Out on a hill at the shepherds' field, the mother ewe, Rechel gathered her twin lambs close beside her for the night. Benjamin sat down beside them and wrapped his wool tunic tightly around his shivering body. He had finished gathering the rest of the sheep and was waiting for his father to come and take his watch of the flock. Benjamin's father seemed later than usual. Rechel wondered what could be keeping him. While they waited, Benjamin took out his reed pipe and began playing a soft melody to calm the restless sheep. His father had made the pipe out of two hollowed-out pieces of cane and had given it to Benjamin when he had come home from Jerusalem. His father had also given him a sling. This was a father's way of telling his son he was man enough to be one of the shepherds who could care for and protect the village flock. After the music had calmed the sheep, Benjamin set his reed pipe down and gazed into the sky. A chilly spring breeze made Rechel shiver. The night air echoed the tinkling bells of the other sheep as they stirred.

Benjamin seemed deep in thought when his father walked from behind and sat beside him on the grassy hillside.

"It is a beautiful night tonight isn't it, son?" his father said.

Benjamin looked at his father and smiled. "Yes, and I was just thinking how wonderful it is to be home again."

"God has been good to us," said Benjamin's father. "I am thankful for the man in Jerusalem who paid our debt so you could return to us."

Benjamin nodded his head and then looked up into the sky again. "They are beautiful aren't they," he said.

The stars twinkled down at them through the crisp night air.

"Yes," said Benjamin's father. He paused for a moment. "It seems one of them is moving toward us."

Suddenly, the sheep on the hillside crowded closer together and moved restlessly in their flock. When Rechel saw the strange light she made sure the twins stayed close to her. The other shepherds on the hillside joined Benjamin and his father.

"What is it?" Benjamin asked his father.

"I know not," his father answered.

The light grew brighter and brighter. All watched in fearful amazement as a light far greater than the sun encompassed them. When from the midst of the light an angel appeared, the shepherds fell on their knees and bowed to the earth.

Suddenly the night became alive with music, and the most wonderful sights Rechel had ever seen. She felt as if she were looking right into heaven. Rechel listened as the angel announced the birth of a new king in Bethlehem.

When the angel disappeared, the shepherds arose. Benjamin's father looked at Benjamin and said, "We must go to Bethlehem and search for the king. What a wonderful thing the Lord has made known to us.

Rechel looked at her twins who were still gazing heavenward at the remaining light that shone in the sky. There was a new star in the heavens with its rays pouring down like sunshine to a particular place on the edge of Bethlehem. Rechel wondered if the light would direct the shepherds to the babe, of whom the angel had spoken.

Rechel and Sarah started to follow Benjamin and the other shepherds when Hanna bleated sadly. She wanted to go with them. Rechel knew she could never make it that far with her crippled leg. More than anything she wanted to see the newborn king but she knew they could not leave Hanna behind. She would have to stay with her. Suddenly Benjamin came running back to Hanna. Quickly, he picked her up in his arms and placed her on his shoulders. Together, they started toward the town of Bethlehem.

22

Men from the East

Baruch slipped through the market place trying to find something to eat. Perhaps he needed to improve his begging skills, he thought to himself. He had not gotten a decent meal for several days and he was starving. He had, however, acquired several bruises from people throwing rocks at him.

With his nose to the ground, he continued sniffing, in hopes that he might find a morsel of food someone had dropped. As Baruch came around the corner of one of the merchant stands, he was surprised to see a group of people gathered around three finely dressed men. Never before had he seen men like these in the marketplace.

Baruch immediately guessed that these men had come from a land far away. One was clothed in a linen robe that was a colorful purple and blue. Another wore a woolen cloak trimmed with the most delicate designs and fringed with soft, dangling tassels. Their gold bracelets had insets of fine jewels. Golden pendants hung from their necks. A crown adorned one man's head. Even the priests who visited the marketplace occasionally to show off their fine clothing were not nearly as well dressed as these men. These were definitely men of power and wealth.

Baruch moved closer to hear what they were saying.

"Where can we find Him, the King of the Jews?" one of the men asked.

A man called to him from the crowd, "Do you seek Herod?"

"We seek a newborn child," the robed man said.

For a moment Baruch forgot about the hunger pain in his stomach. "A child?" he thought. Baruch remembered Yonah and Timothy had told everyone at the stable there would be a special child born that would be a new king. Could it be that these men were seeking that same child?

Suddenly, an old man with a grisly face and one eyelid that drooped lower than the other became very interested in the three strangers. He seemed concerned and paid special attention to the conversation. The old man leaned closer and turned a withered ear to listen. Suddenly, as if frightened, he scurried away toward Herod's palace. As he rounded a corner out of sight, the man looked back over his shoulder as if to make certain nobody had seen him.

Baruch knew the man had to be one of Herod's evil spies. He stood for a moment trying to decide if he should follow the wretched figure or stay with the three men and learn more of this new king. He finally decided he had better stay and find out if this new king was the king Yonah and Timothy had told them about, the one that would come to free his people.

Within a short time, a small group of Roman soldiers and palace dignitaries led by Balbus could be seen working their way through the crowd toward the strangers. As they approached the three men, Baruch's hair bristled in a sharp ridge down his back. As Balbus walked by, Baruch growled. Balbus tried to strike him with the butt end of a spear but Baruch sprang back out of reach.

Baruch could no longer hear the conversation between the men of the palace and the strangers, but he was certain an invitation was being made. In the midst of the soldiers and other men, Baruch noticed the grisly old man. He was nodding and pointing to Herod's palace. While Baruch watched the Roman soldiers escort the three men out of the market, another led the men's camels away. Something smelled rotten, and it wasn't the day-old produce in the market. Baruch followed the Romans, but when they reached the palace gate Baruch could see he would not be able to get inside the well-guarded gate. He turned and ran back toward the city.

When Baruch arrived back at the marketplace, he heard an awful groaning. He suddenly saw Lydia staggering toward him. Her bridle dangled on one ear and her saddle was slightly turned. "You look a little strange," he said. "You're swaying like a sick camel."

"I am a sick camel," She snorted as she leaned one direction, then the other.

"What's wrong with you?" Baruch asked, careful to keep a safe distance from the unstable creature.

"I ate Kemuel's tent and now I have a terminal case of indigestion," Lydia groaned.

Noticing the empty saddle, Baruch asked, "Did you eat Kemuel too?"

"No, I left him back there in nice a patch of thistle. Just because I ate his rotten old tent he wants me dead! He even swore to use my hide to replace his tent. Can you imagine that? I have been overworked and under appreciated," she sobbed, her large eyes filling with tears.

"Well, it is no wonder you are sick, but you need to recover fast so you can help me!"

With her head Lydia flipped a tassel from her face. "I don't give a fig about helping anyone right now. Don't you understand? I'm sick," she groaned.

"Listen, three men have arrived here from a faraway land and they are looking for a king. These men have been escorted to Herod's palace. I'm sure Herod wants to know all he can about this newborn king. You know Herod guards his throne with insane jealousy and will stop at nothing to preserve his crown.

Lydia spit. "A sorry king Herod is. He takes the top prize of the nasty people. What would you have me do?"

"I am going to the temple mount to find Yonah. Do you suppose you could find those handsome male camels that belong to the strangers? They might be at Zebedee's stable."

"Did you say male camels?"

"They are very rich, handsome male camels," answered Baruch. "Certainly you can use your charm to obtain as much information as possible from them. We must find this new king before Herod does."

Lydia fluttered her eyelashes and planted a kiss on Baruch's forehead. "I'm sure I can find them and influence them with my irresistible appeal." With that, her signs of indigestion disappeared. She turned and swung into a steady trot toward Zebedee's stable.

23

A Noble Attempt

Baruch continued on toward the temple to find Yonah. As he trotted around the east wall of the temple mount he saw a goat tethered to a stake in the ground a short distance ahead. As Baruch drew closer, he realized it was the same ornery goat from the stable. Oddly, a red ribbon was attached to one of his horns.

"Well, if it isn't Big Billy," Baruch said.

"The name is Ahaz."

"What are you doing here anyway?" asked Baruch.

"I have been prepared this day to be the people's scapegoat."

"The peoples' what?"

Ahaz looked very solemn when he explained. "I have been chosen to be the people's goat. By the laying on of hands from the priest, I will receive the sins of the people so they can be forgiven and their consciences cleared. I will then be escorted by the priests into the wilderness and released. I will never be allowed to come back to Jerusalem—for if I do the people's sins will not be forgiven. So that everyone will know what I am, I will be marked forever with this red ribbon and kept away from the city."

Baruch looked at the red ribbon tied around the goat's horn. Then he burst out laughing. "And you believe that stuff? You cannot understand how ridiculous that sounds to me."

"You are just a dog," Ahaz bleated angrily. "How could I ever expect you to understand?"

"I just think it's a little strange that the priests think they can give the people's sins away to a goat. Why can't the people take responsibility for their own sins instead of tying them to a goat?"

"It is symbolic."

"Symbolic of what?"

Ahaz did not answer.

"You don't know do you?"

Ahaz turned his back toward Baruch but Baruch walked around to face Ahaz again.

"You have been imprisoned by these silly superstitions that you don't even understand. Why do you subject yourself to this?" asked Baruch. "The priests have gotten so carried away with the busyness of their elaborate ceremonies they have become blind to the real needs of the people."

"And I suppose you know what the people need?" Ahaz sneered.

"I certainly do."

"And what would that be?" Ahaz asked.

"They need a desire to help each other. The priests could try caring for the poor and needy instead of parading around town showing off their fine apparel."

"I can certainly see how that would benefit you. You are always thinking of yourself," retorted Ahaz.

"I'm thinking of you right now," barked Baruch. "I could get you out of this mess."

"No!" answered Ahaz. "This ritual is an honor. I will not neglect my duties."

"Well, I will be on my way then. I guess you wouldn't be interested in saving a new king. That's certainly not as honorable as wandering around in the wilderness with sins stuck on your back and a ribbon tied to your horn."

"What are you talking about?" questioned Ahaz.

"The King, the one Yonah told us about, I think he has been born."

"You should be ashamed of yourself mumbling such blasphemy! There are severe penalties for crimes against blaspheming God."

"Believe what you want, this is not blasphemy. This is the truth. There are three men, and very important men I must add, that have just entered the city. They have come from the east searching for a newborn king. Herod has them at his palace right now. I'm sure he is questioning them at this very moment. You know what Herod will do if he finds this child." Baruch turned to leave.

"Where do you think you are going?" asked Ahaz.

"I am going to the temple pinnacle to find Yonah. He will know what to do to help save this child."

"They will never let your kind inside the temple mount. They will kill you first."

Trotting off on stiff legs and with his head in the air, Baruch called back, "I'm not afraid to die. I know all dogs go to heaven."

When Baruch reached the temple mount he climbed the terraces that led to the east gate and tried to blend into the crowd so he could slip through the temple gate without being seen, but as he started inside the gate, a priest cried, "Get that dog out of here! Dogs are not allowed here!"

Someone reached to strike a blow but missed. Another caught Baruch with his foot and sent him tumbling down the terraces. Baruch yelped in pain and scrambled back to his feet, but then came the rocks and sticks. Finally, he retreated away from the gate and back to the lower city, where he stopped to rest underneath an olive tree. Yonah, soaring high above, flew down and landed by Baruch.

"What manner of mischief are you up to now?"

Baruch licked his wounds. "I was only trying to sneak into the temple."

"Baruch, you are a dog. You are not allowed into the temple," Yonah reminded him.

"Sometimes it isn't easy being a dog," he growled.

"Sometimes it isn't easy having you be a dog," said Yonah.

"I was just trying to do something good."

"The Lord promises those who are good will be blessed."

"I'm not the one who needs the blessings right now. I'm afraid Herod may be plotting something evil.

Yonah tilted his head to one side. "I am aware of the three men at Herod's palace. I followed them to the palace but I too am unable to get inside to find what that evil Herod is planning. Somehow we must find a way in."

"I hope that task is a little easier than me trying to get past the gate into the temple mount," Baruch huffed.

"I was on my way to find Timothy when I saw you in trouble. Timothy will be able to get into the palace."

Baruch rolled over and began laughing. "You think that quivering little mouse will go into Herod's palace?" he howled. "Perhaps he would be better suited to lead a retreat."

"Baruch, where is your faith?"

"I've heard that faith without works is dead. You may find it difficult to get Timothy to do the work—and even if he does, he might end up deader than my faith anyway."

"Stay here and stay out of trouble. I'll find Timothy. We'll meet you back here and get to work."

24

At the Palace

Baruch waited patiently for Yonah. When the dove finally returned, Baruch could not see Timothy anywhere. "Well, where is he?"

"Timothy," said Yonah, "you can come out now."

Timothy scurried out from behind a large bush. "What is so important that you have brought me out here from the safety of the temple?" he asked.

"We have reason to believe the new king may have been born," said Yonah. "Three men traveling from the east have come to Jerusalem looking for him. It is certain that these are righteous men who know and understand Isaiah's prophesies. They have come here hoping to witness the birth of a new king. Herod has ordered these men to be brought to him at the palace so he can question them."

Timothy, showing definite signs of concern, said, "Oh my goodness! That must be why Herod sent for the priests at the temple. I'm sure he wants to know what the scriptures say concerning this child's birth."

Yonah continued. "Herod's mind is polluted with all sorts of evil. There's no telling what he is planning for the child or for these men. Someone needs to get into the palace."

"Yes, they do," agreed Timothy.

"Someone who is brave and willing to protect this child will have to go."

"Exactly," agreed Timothy.

"We need someone very small who can hide in crevices, is gray like the shadows and is as quiet as a mouse."

"Yes," nodded Timothy, quiet as a..."

Baruch watched as Timothy's eyes suddenly widened.

"No! No!" Timothy exclaimed. "Not me. Herod is a bloodthirsty villain. If he catches me in his palace he will feed me to Felix. No, no, please don't ask me to do such a thing!" He began twisting his tail. His whiskers quivered uncontrollably. He pressed his paws together and rocked back and forth.

Baruch looked at Yonah. "I believe I was right, he is squeaking out on us."

"He just needs to get the panic out of his system. He'll be fine," assured Yonah.

"Oh, that's a great idea," Baruch said as he rolled his eyes. "Panic first so you can get it out of your system and then think logically."

"I'm not going," wailed Timothy.

Baruch stood up and towered over Timothy. "Either you go to the palace and find out what Herod is up to, or I'll have you for dinner myself," he growled. He picked up Timothy by the back of the neck and began jogging toward the palace.

"Put him down," ordered Yonah. "This is no way to treat a valiant servant of the Lord."

Giving Timothy a good shake before he dropped him in the dirt, Baruch apologized sarcastically. "I don't know what could have come over me. I guess panic does seem the proper response for one about to save a king."

Timothy emerged from a cloud of dust and brushed himself off. "I can't do this," he squeaked.

"Quit making such a spectacle out of yourself," Yonah firmly told Timothy. "Are you willing to let your fear keep you from serving God? You must meet this trial with courage." Yonah gave Timothy a stern look. "By small and simple ways, great things come to pass. You are a small dormouse, Timothy, but you have a chance to help the new king. The Holy One that will save his people."

Timothy was humbled by Yonah's comments. "I will go to the palace."

"You must be brave," Yonah urged.

"I will," whispered Timothy, still quivering.

"Then we must go now," Yonah said.

Timothy traveled with Yonah and Baruch across the city to Herod's palace. When they reached the gate, Timothy's fears were realized. It was not going to be easy getting inside. Two large, armored soldiers stood grasping long javelins as they guarded the entrance. Timothy was too busy shaking violently to notice the nervous glances Yonah and Baruch gave each other. Baruch whispered to Yonah: "Timothy has a very queer look in his eyes. His whiskers are quivering again. He has begun rocking back and forth again. I'm not sure he is mentally or emotionally ready for this task. I'm afraid he is going to back out on us."

"He'll be fine," assured Yonah.

Timothy was not fine. He was trembling worse than ever. "What are we going to do now?" he gasped.

Yonah tried to comfort Timothy. "Put these fears behind you and the Lord will be your guide," he said. "Baruch and I can distract them while you slip through the gate. Once you are through, run as fast as you can to the palace."

At that moment, Yonah picked up some small stones in his talons and took to the air. Baruch approached the guards and started barking and carrying on wildly. One of the guards tried to chase him away from the gate, but Baruch escaped the blow from the soldier's javelin and led the guard further away from the gate as a second blow was attempted. At the same time, from above,

Yonah dropped a stone on the other guard's head. When the guard looked up, Timothy slipped through the gate. Baruch looked back in time to see the little mouse running in the shadows along the edge of the wall that led straight to the heart of the palace.

25

Back in the Throne Room

Once inside the gates, Timothy realized he wasn't even sure where he needed to be. He quietly followed a long pathway to some terraces that led to two large doors where another guard stood. Timothy's heart sank. Without Baruch and Yonah there to help, how would he ever get past another soldier and into the palace?

He moved further into the shadows to think. As he considered what to do next, he reached into his scrip and retrieved the turquoise gem. Holding it made him feel wiser. Perhaps he could think of a great plan, some way to get past the next guard and into Herod's throne room. Alas, he could think of nothing, so he put the turquoise gem back into his scrip and waited. Timothy closed his eyes. "Please God," he pleaded. "I am just a timid mouse. I want to help, but I am scared and do not know how to get inside."

Just at that moment, Timothy heard giggling and laughter. He opened his eyes to see a group of women making their way toward the entrance. They stopped at the doors and waited for the guard to let them in. Without thinking, Timothy quickly ducked under the long, flowing robes worn by one of the ladies. The guard bowed as he opened the doors and let the women pass.

Once inside the palace, Timothy scurried along beneath the safety of the woman's robe. He had no idea where he was going—or where she was going. He just kept moving as fast as his legs would carry him, so as not to be exposed. It was not until the lady stopped that Timothy was discovered. Not realizing she was no longer walking, Timothy's little legs carried him out from under his cover and right into the midst of the group for all to see.

Only when one of the ladies cried out, "a mouse!" did Timothy stop running. Where? He thought, looking around. By the time he realized the women were all dancing around pointing to him it was too late. The same woman who had unknowingly escorted him into the palace kicked him across the marble floor. He slid wildly, unable to get his legs beneath him and a moment later, he crashed against the far wall. For a brief moment, he lay there stunned. When he realized he was okay, he scurried around the corner to avoid another kicking—or worse.

He found himself in a large corridor with hallways leading in every direction. "I should not have come," he whispered to himself. "I do not know where to go and this dreaded place is home to the wicked cat, Felix." Timothy expected the beast to appear at any moment from one of the nearby hallways. He now faced the most dangerous of all territories. It was one thing to get into the palace but for the first time, he realized he still had to get out.

Each corridor seemed to go on forever. Timothy was not sure which one to take. He worried he would not be able to find the three men in time. He carefully moved down the hallway just to the left of him. He had not gone very far when Balbus stepped from one of the rooms into the hallway. Squeezing himself up next to the wall, Timothy held his breath. Even the sound of his very own heartbeat seemed too noisy. The whiskers on his nose started quivering again. He knew if he made one wrong move he might be discovered, so he clutched his whiskers to stop the quivering. Sweat dripped from is forehead. He felt a burning in the pit of his stomach.

Balbus passed him, and then disappeared down the hallway into another room. Timothy took a deep breath and crept forward in the direction Balbus had gone. Every few steps Timothy would look back over his shoulder to see if he was being watched. His own shadow caused him to jump. Soon, the small mouse could hear muffled voices coming from behind two large cedar doors. His heart nearly stopped and his legs shook so terribly he thought he would not be able to take another step.

"Please, tiny legs," he pleaded. "This is not a time to betray me.

He pressed onward until he reached the doors. One of the doors was slightly ajar and Timothy quietly crept inside and scurried to the edge of the room where he could see who was talking. Suddenly, his eyes grew wide. He had found Herod's throne room. As he looked around the ornate room he was relieved to see Felix was asleep, lying on a Persian rug at Herod's feet. Next to Herod's throne stood Balbus with his arms folded across his broad chest. The three men Yonah had spoken of stood facing Herod. Timothy strained to hear the conversation between the three strangers and King Herod. Herod smiled coldly at the men. "Your presence is my pleasure. I am told you are looking for a new king that might have been born."

The men bowed and then one of them knelt before Herod. "Your Majesty, we are grateful for your invitation to the palace. We have come from afar searching for a child of prophecy. No one in Jerusalem seems to know of the child.. We hoped you might know where he can be found.

"This is a question for those who study the prophesies in the scriptures. Fortunately for you, I have questioned the priests and scribes from the temple. They tell me this child of prophecy will be born in the City of David, which is Bethlehem. But they know of no such child having been born."

"The signs in the heavens lead us to believe the time has come for his birth. We have come to worship him."

Herod's face grew impatient. "Go then and find him!" he snapped.

The three men looked at one another and then the one who had knelt before Herod earlier said, "Your Majesty, we thank you for your help. We will be on our way." Together, they turned to leave.

Herod stood and followed the three men toward the door where Balbus stood. "Wait. I have been a little sharp with you, my kind friends," he said. "Please forgive me. When you find this young child, come and tell me where he is, so that I may go and worship him also."

Timothy watched as the men were escorted out of the throne room. Once they had left, Herod turned to Balbus and handed him several gold coins. "Follow those men. Find the child and kill him." Balbus nodded and with a grim smile on his face, dropped the coins into his pocket and left the room.

Timothy's blood turned cold. How could Herod possibly do such a thing? Timothy suddenly knew his only hope for this child's safety was to get back to Yonah and Baruch and tell them of Herod's plans. It was time to find his way back out of the palace.

As Timothy turned to leave, a large dark shadow fell across his path. Timothy froze. Even without looking, he knew Felix had awoken and found him. He could feel the cat's hot breath on the back of his neck. Timothy had been so focused on the three men and Herod that he hadn't realized that Felix was no longer sleeping on the rug.

Timothy whirled and faced the cat. The cat's eyes narrowed as he prepared to pounce. His tasseled black ears lay flat against his head and his stubby tail flicked back and forth. His deadly teeth flashed.

Timothy was overcome by terror. He knew he could not outrun the cat. As Felix sprang Timothy jumped aside. Felix managed to swat Timothy with his mighty paw and he sent the dormouse flying into the throne room.

Timothy wasted no time scrambling to his feet. He immediately ran for a nearby table covered with a linen cloth. Hoping to evade the cat long enough to get back out of the room he darted underneath the table. Felix sunk his claws into the linen cloth and pulled it from the table, bringing with it the meat Herod had been eating and the cup of wine Herod had been drinking prior to his visitors' arrival. Timothy was now exposed.

Herod stood from his throne and yelled, "Get those animals out of here!" Guards hurried toward the table as Timothy fled to the other side of the room. In the commotion, Timothy scrambled frantically to reach the rug at the far side of the room near the window. He disappeared underneath the rug near Herod's throne. Felix pounced again, clawing at the rug and ripping it to pieces. Timothy frantically tried to get away. He had never moved so quickly in his entire life. He shot out from under the rug only to find himself at the feet of Herod. Timothy heard the hiss of the cat and turned to run. In an instant, Felix followed, crashing into Herod's feet, knocking the king's legs out from under him. As Herod fell to the floor, he screamed, "Kill them! Kill them both!"

As Felix tried to untangle himself from his master's legs, Timothy raced toward the door as quickly as he could, expecting at any moment to feel the crushing blow of the cat upon him.

Timothy reached the partially open door of the throne room and slipped through it. At that very instant Felix crashed into the doors causing them to close. Felix hissed and screamed angrily as he clawed at the doors trying to get them open.

Timothy had survived for the moment, but suddenly realized he was still in desperate trouble. His scrip was caught in the closed doors. He tugged furiously, but he realized that the precious stone inside the scrip was preventing him from pulling it between the closed doors. "No!" he cried, not wanting to let go.

On the other side, Felix howled furiously and Timothy could hear footsteps quickly advancing.

Frantically he pulled at the scrip, but it did not come free. Timothy thought about letting go and running for his life, but he couldn't leave the stone. Desperately, he tugged downward on the scrip, until finally he managed to coax it to the bottom of the door. Pulling with all of his strength he freed the scrip from beneath the door. As he raced down the dimly lit hallway looking for a way out, he reached inside his scrip and made sure the precious stone was still safe. He turned a corner, then another. The sounds of the hissing cat and the footsteps seemed to be going a different direction. Timothy tried to think.

He was sure that the cat would be looking for him and it was only a matter of time before the caracal found him again. He tried going down several different corridors, but each one led to a locked door. What if he didn't get out? What would happen to the new king? Would Herod find him first? Timothy wrung his tail and rocked back and forth. How did he get involved with this anyway? Why did he have to see the angel? He reached into his scrip, pulled out the stone and began rubbing it. It was so beautiful, but he had almost lost it. Now all he wanted was to get back to the temple and quietly go about his business. But that was impossible. He put the gem back into his scrip. How was he going to get out and warn the others?

As he sat there thinking, Timothy felt a slight breeze blowing down the hallway and suddenly he detected the smell of fresh flowers. His whiskers twitched as he followed the breeze to an open doorway that led to a courtyard surrounded by a beautiful garden. Across the courtyard a rock wall rose up before him. Somewhere in that wall there had to be a gate. If he could make it across the courtyard to the wall he was sure he could follow the wall until he found the gate. Once he found the gate, he could sneak out. He stopped for a moment to catch his breath and control his shaking. His legs felt weak and he was a still a little dizzy from so much running. Timothy moved on toward the palace wall.

He quickly followed the wall. Finally, he could see the gate leading out of the palace courtyard. It wasn't far and he only had to get past one guard who seemed to be preoccupied with shining his sword. On the other side of the wall was freedom and safety. To Timothy's pleasant surprise, the guard did not notice him as he quietly slipped through the gate. He was relieved to finally be outside the palace wall. He had made it!

Timothy breathed a sigh of relief. After he leaned against the outside of the wall for a moment to catch his breath, he started off to find Baruch and Yonah. He had gone only a short distance when he stopped. The hair on his back tingled. Something was not right. He felt that same hot breath on the back of his neck. Slowly he turned around and looked back. Felix had found him. Timothy shrieked and made a valiant attempt to flee, but Felix slammed a paw down on Timothy's tail. "Your mine now," he snarled. "You will not escape me again!"

26

Yonah's Brave Stand

Timothy struggled desperately to get loose but was unable to free himself. Felix, holding Timothy's tail with his right paw, batted him back and forth with his left paw, "What were you doing in Herod's palace," he questioned.

"Nothing," Timothy answered.

Felix batted Timothy back and forth again, "You would not have left the safety of the temple and ventured into Herod's palace for nothing, " he snarled.

Timothy tried again to free himself from Felix's grasp. "Let me go! Let me go!"

Felix let go of Timothy then quickly grabbed him again. Slowly he unsheathed a single claw and ran it underneath Timothy's chin. "Would you like to try answering my question correctly this time? What were you doing in Herod's palace?"

Timothy had no intention of giving Felix the information he was seeking. He knew Felix would not release him even if he told Felix why he had come to the palace. Exhausted with this cat and mouse game Timothy pleaded. "Please, I can't take anymore."

Felix curled back his lips and exposed his sharp teeth. "Fine," he hissed, "I can see you are of no more use to me."

So this is how it ends, thought Timothy. Like so many others before him, he would know the pain and terror of falling victim to the cruel Felix. He had tried to do the right thing, but he had failed. Shaking violently he closed his eyes and prepared for the fatal bite.

Because his eyes were closed, Timothy wasn't sure what happened next, but he heard Felix hiss and when he opened his eyes he saw a flurry of white feathers soaring toward them.

"Yonah!" cried Timothy.

Yonah swooped down and struck the cat on the head. For a moment, Felix dropped Timothy and turned his attention to the dove that had just attacked him from above. Timothy took advantage of the distraction and started running. There was no time to lose. The dove was flapping wildly just beyond the reach of the cat. Felix did not waste too much time on Yonah, however. He quickly turned and caught Timothy by the tail once more.

Again, Yonah struck the cat from behind. Felix swiped the air with one paw, but his strokes were rendered ineffective because his grip on Timothy required the other paw to stay on the ground.

Timothy cried out, "Help! Help!"

Yonah immediately plunged into a full-power dive.

Timothy felt Felix release him. "No!" cried Timothy.

But it was too late. Felix crouched on his hind legs and as the churning mass of white feathers came down toward him, he sprang. Before Yonah could pull out of the dive, Felix caught him with his front paw and hurled Yonah against the rock wall.

Timothy wanted to run, but he couldn't. Felix now turned his full attention to the injured bird. Yonah tried to fly but couldn't because one wing hung awkwardly at his side. Felix crept slowly and deliberately toward the dove.

Finding courage he didn't know he had, Timothy seized Felix by the hind leg and with all his strength bit into the cat. Felix kicked Timothy loose and moved on. Killing doves was the cat's real sport.

"No!" Timothy cried. "No!" Timothy struck the cat in the face with his scrip.

Felix was not distracted. His focus was on the helpless bird.

Yonah called to Timothy. "Timothy, leave me. Run away from here and warn the others!"

Timothy knew he should get away, but he couldn't bring himself to turn and flee. "I can't leave you!" he squeaked.

When Felix was nearly upon Yonah he hesitated for a moment. "I recognize you," he snarled. "You are the one that escaped from the Arena of the Caracal Cats, but I shall have my complete victory at last and leave you dead at the feet of Herod, my master."

Suddenly, Timothy heard a sharp bark and from out of nowhere, Baruch appeared. He charged Felix, knocking him away from Yonah. "Back off, you slant-eyed foot-licking meowling! Pick on someone your own size!"

"Stay out of this you mongrel!" Felix hissed as he leaped toward Baruch. With claws unsheathed, he lashed out and tore open Baruch's shoulder.

Baruch lunged at the cat, but the more agile Felix leaped out of the way and seized Baruch from behind. Baruch managed to shake him loose. Baruch lunged again, and again Felix raked the dog with his claws, this time across the nose. Baruch let out a yelp, but was not deterred. As he faced the cat again, his hair bristled and a deep growl rose from his throat.

Baring his sharp teeth, the cat circled, looking for another opening. Baruch continued to stay face to face with Felix. Pound for pound, even Baruch was no match for this large angry caracal. However, retreating was not an option.

Finally, the cat reared up and attacked in full force, gnashing and snarling. Blood and fur filled the air as Felix and Baruch rolled in a tangled mass, locked furiously in combat. The ugly battle continued until Baruch sank his teeth deep into the cat's shoulder and threw him to the ground. He tried to maintain his grip but the cat was too strong. With powerful strength, Felix broke loose from Baruch's grasp. His tail dropped low to the ground and his ears flattened as he backed away from the dog. When he was safely out of Baruch's reach, Felix spun on his hind legs and raced back through the palace gate.

"I guess I put that paw licker in his place," boasted Baruch.

"Don't be so sure of yourself," came a voice from behind. "He knew he couldn't beat us both."

Baruch turned and looked back. "Well if it isn't Big Billy."

"The name is Ahaz," the goat grumbled, "and I'm warning you he'll be back."

"I hope he does come back." Baruch sat down and began licking his wounds.

"I'd love to sink my teeth into that hairball again," he said. "How did you get in here anyway, you old pickle sucker?" he asked. "I thought you were out in the desert packing around everyone's sins."

Luckily for you I showed up to save your hide."

"I didn't need your help," growled Baruch. "I could have handled him myself."

"I'm sure you will get another chance. Felix doesn't take defeat so lightly. It will be a miracle if any of us manage to get out of here alive."

"You really have an incredible ability to take a bad situation and make it worse," barked Baruch. "You could be a little more positive."

"I am being realistic," said Ahaz flatly.

"Please!" Timothy interrupted in a panic. "Yonah is hurt. We need to stop this bickering and get out of here before that cat decides to come back!"

Suddenly, the sound of people could be heard shouting nearby.

"It's time to go," said Ahaz.

"Why are those people shouting?" asked Baruch.

"Don't you remember me telling you? I am not allowed back in the city. The priests are looking for me. Let's go!"

"Leave me here," insisted Yonah. "I am badly injured. I will only be a burden in my condition. I'm afraid I might be dying. At least I can detain Felix for a short time."

"No, no!" wailed Timothy. "You will be alright."

"We will not leave you here to be a sacrifice for us," argued Ahaz.

Ahaz spun around, "Quickly, follow me."

27

The Way Out

Baruch picked Yonah up tenderly in his mouth and followed Ahaz. Timothy scurried behind as fast as he could but he could not keep up with the others.

"Wait for me!" yelled Timothy.

Ahaz stopped, whirled around and came back to help Timothy. "Hop on my back and I'll carry you. But hurry. We have no time to lose."

Timothy pulled himself up onto Ahaz's back. Together they made their way through the narrow streets back toward the city.

By the time they reached the city Baruch realized that Yonah was growing weaker by the minute.

Baruch stopped near a merchant stand next to a mountain of brightly colored cloth. He carefully set Yonah on the ground. "Yonah needs to rest," he said.

Timothy jumped from Ahaz's back and they all gathered around Yonah.

"You must be committed to find the child," Yonah managed to say. "Promise me, you will not give up." Then he closed his eyes and lay very still.

"Please don't die," pleaded Timothy. "We need your help."

"Now what are we going to do?" asked Ahaz, turning toward Baruch. "We will never be able to find the king. Yonah is the only one who knows the prophesies of Isaiah."

From the mound of cloth came a familiar voice. "Oh, the mere mention of Isaiah makes my heart dance!"

"I think I know those gurgling bellows," said Baruch as he trotted over and pulled away a piece of cloth from the mound. Lydia poked her head out and kissed him on the nose. She was lying down underneath the pile of cloth.

Baruch turned to Ahaz and smiled, "Isn't she lovely?"

"That is not how I would describe her," Ahaz grumbled.

"Lydia," said Baruch, "it is good to see you. What are you doing under there?"

"I'm hiding."

"Why are you hiding?" asked Timothy.

Kemuel found me at Zebedee's stable and he is chasing me. I refuse to end up as part of his new tent."

"What news do you bring us from Zebedee's stable?" asked Baruch.

Lydia's big brown eyes looked straight at Baruch as if she did not understand the question.

"Don't you remember?" he reminded. "I sent you there to find the camels of the three men."

Lydia fluttered her long eyelashes. "Oh yes, let me think." She looked upward to the left, then to the right as she tilted her head first one way, then the other, obviously trying mightily to remember if she had completed the important task she had been given.

"Well, don't think too hard," grumbled Ahaz, "You might hurt your brain. "

"Listen, you old goat," Baruch growled. "She's probably a little confused and tired from being chased all day by Kemuel."

"Ah, yes." Lydia smiled at Baruch, "I found the other camels. They were handsome creatures and we had a wonderful conversation!"

"What did they tell you about the new king they have been searching for?" asked Baruch.

Lydia paused for a moment and gave Baruch a blank stare. "I don't remember; in fact, I'm not sure I remembered to ask them that question."

Ahaz rolled his eyes upward. "This predicament is more serious than I had imagined," he groaned. "We have a bird that is barely alive, a terrified mouse, a fugitive camel with no memory, and a dog who has no sense of responsibility." He began walking away from the group.

"There is no reason for such rudeness," said Lydia.

"That's right," barked Baruch. "Not all of us are perfect enough to have a red ribbon tied to our horns and sent off into the wilderness to carry everyone else's sins."

Ahaz spun around and went face to face with Baruch. "Is that sarcasm I hear flickering in my ears?" he bleated.

"I just tell it how I see it," retorted Baruch.

Timothy put his hands over his ears and cried out. "Stop! I don't want to hear any more. We need to continue on our way in search of the king. That is what Yonah wants us to do."

"It might help if someone knew where we were going," mumbled Ahaz.

"Let's just go back to Zebedee's stable and ask the camels ourselves," suggested Timothy.

"And how do you suppose we are going to get out of here?" asked Ahaz.

Baruch sat for a moment and began to analyze the situation then he looked at Lydia. "Lydia, you beautiful flower of the desert, can you help me get us back to Zebedee's stable?"

Lydia shook off the remaining piece of cloth from her head. With her head held high she said, "Let me point out to you, I have traveled across vast stretches of wilderness for weeks in the scorching sun without so much as a sip of water. With heavy packs I have walked through blowing sand dunes and climbed hundreds of steep, rocky, mountains. I have endured driving rainstorms and flash floods. I am the ship of the desert."

"For heavens sake," interrupted Ahaz. "You are a camel and we are only going to Zebedee's stable. Anyway, I'm not sure we can trust this dog."

"I'm going with Baruch," assured Lydia. "He knows this city better than anyone."

"We will need to put Timothy and Yonah in your saddle pack so they will be safe," explained Baruch. "Then we can travel faster."

Baruch carefully picked Yonah up in his mouth and tucked him into Lydia's saddle pack. Timothy climbed in with Yonah.

Ahaz looked at Baruch and said, "I want you to know I'm not one bit happy with this situation but I guess we are stuck with each other until this mission is finished."

"You can certainly stay here if you like. I'm sure you're not worried about being left alone here with that cat on the roof of that building staring right at you. I guess you haven't noticed he has been following us since we left Herod's palace. Oh, and the priests over there looking for a goat with a red ribbon, are heading this way."

"I'm not afraid of that cat or the priest but I better go with you," informed Ahaz. "You will need someone like me who can handle some responsibility."

Baruch looked at Lydia and said, "Alright, my long-legged beauty you know what to do."

"Of course," Lydia answered as she heaved herself to her feet with a groan. "Let's go!"

With Baruch in the lead, the band of fugitives darted from the narrow street. Winding his way through the city Baruch led them down one narrow street and then another toward Zebedee's stable. Occasionally he caught sight of Felix leaping from one roof to the next. Baruch knew the cat would continue to pursue them. Whatever happened, he vowed with his life to honor the wishes of Yonah. Somehow he would find the newborn king. But right now, he just needed to get everyone safely out of the city and back to Zebedee's stable.

Up ahead, Baruch saw an opening that led to the east gate of the city wall. It was time to get out of the narrow streets where they risked getting trapped. They were almost there when Kemuel, waving a very large stick stepped into the street blocking their way to the opening.

"Lydia! You sour old tent tarp! I have you now!" he cried.

28

On to Bethlehem!

To avoid any conflict with Kemuel, Baruch slid to a stop and turned around looking for another way out. Baruch heard Kemuel's stick crash down behind him, but it missed. Lydia was not as agile as Baruch and could not get stopped in time. Kemuel waved his stick and jumped wildly from one foot to the other. At the last possible moment he jumped out of the way to avoid being trampled. Kemuel shouted revenge as Lydia slid past him and turned to follow Baruch. Baruch looked back to make sure everyone was still with him.

To complicate matters, now at the other end of the street, a merchant pulling a small brown cart blocked the road. The cart was loaded with several cages.

Baruch ran around the cart but Lydia was too big, so she tried to jump over it. Instead, she caught her foot on one of the cages and knocked it to the ground. She stumbled over it but quickly regained her balance and continued on. As Ahaz came along, he hooked the contraption with his horn and sent the cage flying through the air. When it landed, it broke into pieces. From the broken cage staggered a fat little hen and an old rooster.

Baruch heard the hen clucking furiously to the stunned rooster, "Come on Ezra! Run!"

The old pair of chickens joined the rest of the group, running as fast as they could to keep up with the others.

Baruch led the animals down another street and out of the city gate trying to put some distance between themselves and their pursuers. Once they were outside of the city walls they stopped for a moment to catch their breath. Baruch looked at Ahaz and asked, "Are you happy yet?"

Ahaz didn't answer. He just shook his head and trotted off toward Zebedee's stable. The rest followed.

When they reached Zebedee's stable Baruch looked around but saw no sign of the three camels of which Lydia had spoken. Eli the ox stood quietly at the far end of Zebedee's stable, a large wooden yoke slung across his neck.

"Eli," Baruch asked, "Where are the camels?"

"I'm afraid they have gone," replied Eli.

Baruch looked at Lydia. She hung her head in disappointment. "I am sorry," she said softly to the others. "I thought they would still be here in the stable."

"Great, now we'll never find them," grumbled Ahaz.

Baruch shot a sideways glance at Ahaz and then turned back to Eli. "Why are you still wearing a yoke around your neck?" he asked.

Eli lifted his head and said matter-of-factly, "Zebedee will be back soon to get me to finish some work at the quarry. Besides, I like this yoke. It was specially made for me."

"It's beautiful!" exclaimed Lydia.

Baruch shook his head. "It looks heavy," he said.

"It is heavy but I feel it a privilege to wear it. It represents my responsibility and the burden I bear as the lead ox at the quarry."

Just then Timothy emerged from Lydia's saddle pack. "Is it safe to come out now?"

"You are always safe with me," Lydia said.

Eli looked toward the doorway where two ragged-looking chickens huddled closely together. "I see you have brought along some new friends," said the ox.

All of the animals turned to look at the two stragglers.

Ahaz walked over to them. "Who are you?" he asked sternly.

"I am Naomi," the hen clucked, "and this is Ezra. He has lost his voice and can't crow anymore. I haven't produced an egg for months so we were on our way to the market to be sold for stew meat. I dare say that you have saved us from some dreadful consequences."

"Oh, you poor things," Lydia sniffled. "You must come with us." She kissed Naomi on the head.

"Where are you going?" asked Naomi.

"We are searching for the new king," answered Lydia.

Timothy scurried up onto Lydia's hump. "Herod wants the child dead," he squeaked. "He has sent the Roman soldier Balbus to kill him. We must find him before Balbus discovers his whereabouts."

Baruch sat down and began scratching behind his ear. "Unfortunately, we have no idea where to look," he said. "We were hoping the three men and their camels could lead us to him. But they have already gone."

Lydia looked hopefully at Baruch. "You are a dog. You have a keen sense of smell. Track them," she said. "If anyone can do it, you can."

Baruch lifted his head and began sniffing the air. "All I can smell is that odorous goat."

Ahaz lowered his head, "Why you—"

"Bethlehem," interrupted Eli.

Baruch turned to the ox and asked. "What did you say?"

"Bethlehem," said Eli again. "When the men came to get their camels I heard them say they were going to Bethlehem."

"That makes perfect sense!" exclaimed Timothy. "I remember hearing Herod tell the men at the palace that his priests had informed him of a royal child that was prophesied in the Holy Scriptures. The scriptures say the child will be born in the City of David which is Bethlehem."

"If the priests know of no such child, maybe there isn't one," snorted Ahaz.

"What would Herod's priests know?" asked Baruch sarcastically. "They think they can give their sins to a goat."

Ahaz ignored Baruch. "The city is extremely crowded and certainly it will be impossible for us to find such a child."

"Yonah asked us not to give up searching for this king, and for Yonah's sake, I will honor that request," said Baruch. "The child's life is in danger. I'm going to Bethlehem to search for him."

"And I am going with Baruch," spat Lydia.

"We must hurry," squeaked Timothy.

"I would be honored to accompany you as well," Eli said. The large yoke still hung around his strong neck.

"Well," snorted Ahaz, "I do not plan on staying here alone with two fugitive chickens!"

"Oh, we are not staying here," clucked Naomi.

"Then let's go!" barked Baruch! "We must make it to the City of David before Balbus."

Holding his head high, he trotted out of the stable. With the sound of hooves clomping along behind him, he led the animals from Jerusalem on the road toward Bethlehem.

29

The Light

They had not gone very far when Timothy poked his head out of the saddlebags and called to Baruch "Are we there yet?" he questioned.

"Are we there yet?" grumbled Ahaz. "We don't even know where we are going. How could we possibly be there yet?"

"We are going to Bethlehem," Baruch barked.

"And when we get to Bethlehem have you decided just where in Bethlehem we are going?" questioned Ahaz.

Baruch knew the animals needed reassured they would find the new king but he could not answer Ahaz. Daylight was fading and in a short time darkness would overcome them. Suddenly, Timothy raised a cry of alarm. "The cat! The cat is still following us!" squeaked Timothy as he ducked back down into the saddlebags.

Quickly, Baruch glanced in the direction Timothy had pointed. The hair on the back of Baruch's neck bristled. He was hoping

Felix had given up the chase. When he caught a glimpse of the fearsome beast trailing alongside them he said, "Stay close together. This cat has kept his distance in the daylight, but with nightfall coming he will wait for someone to fall behind and then he will strike."

"I'll just stomp him in the ground if he tries anything!" bellowed Lydia.

"He would be a fool to attack us while we are all together," commented Eli.

Baruch knew that Felix would defend his territory with a vengeance and would stalk endlessly any enemy that had trespassed into his realm. With Timothy and Yonah tucked safely in Lydia's pack, Ahaz or himself would be the cat's first target.

Everyone huddled closer together and moved onward. Except for the sound of the animals' hooves, the road to Bethlehem seemed fairly quiet. It was almost too quiet. Baruch knew that Felix was out there somewhere waiting for the right time to attack. Baruch watched closely for any sign of Felix. He hadn't seen the cat for some time. He would have been less nervous if he had seen him and knew where he was lurking.

Eli suddenly slowed to a stop. "That is very strange," he said. "Isn't there too much light in the sky for this time of night?"

"Yes, you're right," replied Baruch. "It's coming from that star. I have never noticed that star in the heavens before."

Timothy poked his head out of Lydia's saddlebag to look at the star. "It's amazing!" he said as he gazed at the light in the sky.

"Well I've seen the star before," exclaimed Lydia.

Baruch suddenly became interested in what Lydia was telling them. "When did you see it?" he asked.

"I didn't actually see it," Lydia answered. "Those three male camels told me about the star. They have been following it. They said you couldn't see it in the daylight and I forgot to look at night."

Baruch had a strange feeling that the star might have something to do with finding the King. "What else did they tell you about the star?" he asked.

"I don't remember."

"How long has it been there?"

"I don't remember."

"What do you remember," Ahaz mumbled to himself.

Baruch looked up and studied the light in the sky. "The light is descending on the bluff outside of the city wall," he said.

"Maybe it will lead us to the king we are seeking," said Eli.

Suddenly, Baruch was distracted by a shadow that fell across an opening between two large rocks. Then it was gone.

30

The Final Chase

Baruch raised his nose to the air and sniffed the breeze, but smelled nothing. Because of the light, the shadows had almost fled entirely. As they continued on their way, Baruch watched for any sign of movement in the trees and rocks along the road. He hoped that with the light from the star Felix would find it more difficult to make himself invisible.

In an effort to get everyone to move more quickly toward the safety of the city wall Baruch called out, "We must hurry!"

Up ahead, he could see that the road curved slightly as it followed the low contour of the hillside. Baruch could not see around the bend in the road because of the hill and it made him nervous. He knew that Felix could easily wait for them as they came around the curve and they would not be able to see him until it was too late. Baruch found it difficult to catch any foreboding scent on the air, but his instinct warned him of some danger that lurked.

As the animals rounded the bend in the road, Baruch could see an old olive tree, its thick trunk supporting several gnarled arms that reached upward until they disappeared into a tangle of leaves and branches that extended over the road. Large boulders lay strewn along the edge of the road and Baruch watched for any sign of the angry cat, but he saw nothing that looked out of the ordinary.

Baruch looked back at the others. The old hen Naomi, clucked along, flapped her wings and tried to keep up with the others. Baruch barked at her to hurry and to stay close. Timothy was poking his head out of Lydia's saddlebag still watching the light in the sky. Ahaz was trotting along with his usual scowl. Eli and the others moved along unsuspecting of any trouble.

As they came to the tree, Baruch sensed that something was terribly wrong. The wind shifted a little and Baruch was certain that Felix was nearby.

The quiet of the night was suddenly interrupted by the sound of horse hooves pounding down the road behind them. Baruch looked back and saw Balbus as he galloped Keezhar at full speed around the bend. His red cloak flowed behind him snapping in the wind. Every one of the animals scattered off the road and hid as he raced past.

Baruch barked furiously, "Back to the road! Stay together! Felix is still out there somewhere. Hurry we don't have much time. Balbus is moving toward the city. We must follow him and make sure he will not find the new king."

The animals quickly moved back together and when all were accounted for Baruch led them on a run after Balbus. Naomi and Ezra were having some trouble keeping up with the others.

Baruch, fearing Ezra and Naomi would fall prey to Felix, stopped. "Whoa," he said. "We cannot leave these two behind! Quickly," Baruch ordered. "Lydia, let them on your back!"

Lydia dropped down to her side. Once Naomi and Ezra were on her back she heaved herself up and they were on their way again. They reached the edge of the city but could not see Balbus anywhere. There were too many people and the city was extremely crowded.

Baruch was about to lead the animals down the city streets when suddenly he spotted the familiar uniform of a Roman soldier at the entrance to a nearby inn. He was talking to a man who appeared to be the innkeeper. The man shook his head and pointed down the road toward a small cave-like stable. As the soldier turned, Baruch recognized Balbus. Without a word, the Roman swung himself onto Keezhar's back and galloped down the road toward the stable.

31

Surprise at the Stable

Baruch raced after the Roman. "I've got to stop Balbus," he barked to the other animals. He left the group and raced after Balbus.. When Baruch neared the stable he could see the soldier dismounting in a cloud of dust. His red cloak snapped in the breeze. As Balbus disappeared into the cave, Baruch's heart raced. "There's still time," he told himself, hoping that he wasn't too late. He did not have much further to go. He ran as fast as he could, teeth bared, ready to fight.

When he finally reached the entrance to the stable, Baruch scrambled headlong into the cave, expecting to catch Balbus in the middle of some horrible deed. Instead, to his utter surprise, Baruch saw the soldier kneeling next to a small manger. The sight of seeing the Roman on his knees was enough to stop Baruch in his tracks. What was happening? Baruch stared in disbelief. He was confused. This was not what he had expected. Cautiously, Baruch crept forward, keeping his eye on the soldier. As he moved closer, he saw a little baby lying quietly in the manger. At that moment Baruch suddenly felt a wave of calm come over him, a feeling of peace like he had never felt before. Balbus no longer seemed a threat. For the first time since he had entered the stable, Baruch looked around. He had been so focused on stopping Balbus that he hadn't realized that there were others quietly watching nearby. Another man, whom Baruch immediately recognized as the same Joseph he encountered in Jerusalem, kneeled with a young mother next to the makeshift cradle, opposite Balbus. Nearby, Joseph's little donkey, Heber lay quietly gazing upon the scene. Baruch continued to search the room. His heart leaped at the sight of three finely dressed men and their camels lying nearby, but he was not surprised to see them. After all, it was these very men that the animals believed would lead them to the new king.

On the far wall, a young shepherd boy stood with several other shepherds. Near him stood a familiar ewe with her twin lambs. Baruch realized it was Rechel from Zebedee's stable.

Nobody seemed concerned about the Roman soldier in their midst. Everybody was gazing toward the center of the stable where the babe lay swaddled in the manger. A soft warm light filled the cave and seemed to gather around the child.

Baruch had never remembered feeling so calm, or so full of joy at the sight of another being. Baruch knew this was no ordinary child. This child was special. Baruch sat down to soak up the wonderful moment.

Suddenly, the doorway to the stable was filled with the figure of a large camel. Baruch turned to see Lydia panting heavily with Timothy still in the saddlebag and two chickens clinging to her back. Right next to her stood Ahaz and Eli. When Lydia stepped through the entryway her eyes grew wide as she saw the newborn baby lying in the manger. Reverently, she knelt down on the floor of the stable. Naomi clucked quietly as she and Ezra hopped down from Lydia's back. Timothy, crawled quietly out of his hiding place, clasped his hands together and smiled. Baruch had been so focused on stopping Balbus, he had almost forgotten the other animals trying to keep up with him. Now that they had arrived, he felt as if everything would be all right. The anxiety of the day fled. The exhaustion from the long journey, the fear of not arriving in time seemed to melt away. Now, everything was calm. Everything was bright. Baruch felt so happy that everyone had made it to the stable safely. Their search for the king was over. They had found Him.

32

The Gift of the King

Baruch watched as the three finely dressed men stepped forward. Without a word, they bowed down and knelt in front of the child. One of the men pulled a beautiful bag from inside his curious robes. As the man opened the bag and laid it before the child, Baruch could see it was filled with pure gold. The other two men brought forth a finely crafted box and opened it near the manger. The rich aroma of frankincense and myrrh floated through the room.

Who could these men be? Baruch silently wondered to himself, marveling at their mysteriousness and generosity. One by one each man paid silent tribute to the child, smiled at the mother and nodded at Joseph.

Time stood still as everybody in the stable basked in the overwhelming feeling of peace and joy. Nobody was in a hurry to leave. When Balbus finally stood and slowly moved away from the cradle, Baruch marveled that he felt no more anger toward the Roman, nor did he feel threatened by the man. Baruch watched as the soldier reached into his pocket and removed a handful of gold coins, which he graciously handed to Joseph. No words were spoken between the two men, but Baruch saw their faces and he understood what was said. Then Balbus turned. It was at that moment that Baruch noticed the ugly scar had disappeared from the soldier's face. In fact, his whole countenance was changed. His once cold, dark eyes were filled with a new light. As he stepped away from the child, Balbus paused and placed his hand on the young shepherd boy's shoulder. The two smiled at each other and nodded.

The shepherd boy reached down and took a bell from each of his sheep. Gently, he moved toward the makeshift cradle and placed the bells next to the manger. He too smiled at Joseph and the young mother. Joseph looked at the young man and returned the smile, a look of recognition and happiness in his eyes. Rechel and her twins followed the boy, pausing at the manger to look upon the child. It was then that Baruch remembered Hanna from Zebedee's stable in Jerusalem. She couldn't walk. She had to be carried everywhere. Yet as surely as he stood there watching, the young lamb was walking without help. Her leg was no longer crippled.

Just then, from the far side of the stable, a gray horse moved quietly toward the manger. It was Keezhar. He had been silently watching from a distance. Baruch felt his heart soften as the large horse gently extended his velvety nose and nuzzled the baby boy. After a moment, Keezhar turned his head and looked at Heber. Baruch saw their eyes meet and then Keezhar lowered his head. As Balbus led Keezhar out of the stable Baruch realized that Keezhar's coat was no longer gray. Instead, his coat gleamed pure white.

Others in the room began to come forward. Lydia, Ahaz, and Eli, found their way to the young child and looked at him in amazement.

Lydia laid her head near the baby, her long eyelashes brushing against his soft cheeks. As she raised her head, a brightly colored tassel that had loosened from her bridle floated down and landed near the newborn king.

Ahaz did not seem his usual grumpy self as he stepped forward, his eyes fixed on the child before him. Baruch watched the old goat carefully and sensed a powerful struggle was taking place within Ahaz. Slowly, Ahaz lowered his head until his horn caught the edge of the manger. Ever so gently he slid the ribbon from his horn, where it lay near the feet of the newborn king. The red ribbon weighed next to nothing, but Baruch could tell by looking at the expression on the goat's face that a huge burden had been lifted from Ahaz.

It was Eli's turn. The strong Ox who had carried his yoke all the way from Jerusalem slowly dropped to his knees and let the wooden yoke he had been carrying slide down his neck until it rested on the floor next to the cradle. After a moment, he raised his head and took a long look at the child. Baruch wondered to himself how strong and gentle Eli was, all at the same time. Nearby, Joseph looked at the yoke and smiled.

By this time, Naomi and Ezra had already made their way to the manger and the two were sitting silently in the nearby straw. Suddenly, a look of surprise came over the hen. As Naomi stood and looked beneath her, Baruch could see a perfect white egg lying in the straw where the old hen had been sitting. She looked at Ezra and clucked, but Ezra just blinked in amazement. After a moment, it became clear that Ezra wanted to leave something as well. Without a sound, he plucked the longest, brightest, and most beautiful feather from his tail and laid it next to Naomi's egg near the manger.

Finally, it was Timothy's turn. Quietly, he scuttled up to the edge of the manger and peered inside. The little mouse gazed down on the child in wonder and seemed to be thinking about something. At last, he gently reached into his leather scrip and pulled out his beautiful stone. He held it in his hands for a moment, and then gently placed it at the head of the manger. Timothy looked completely at ease.

Suddenly, there was a slight movement near the entryway to the stable. Baruch turned to see the figure of a large cat. It was Felix. His tufted ears lay flat against his neck and his eyes were fixed on the little dormouse. He was ready to spring. Baruch had been so focused on the child and everybody else in the stable that he had completely forgotten about the ever-lurking cat. Instinctively, Baruch started to move between Felix and Timothy but he didn't need to, because as soon as Felix moved into the soft glow of the light surrounding the manger something amazing happened. It seemed the cat had suddenly forgotten about the fat little dormouse perched on the edge of the manger. Instead, Felix rose from his crouched position and gazed at the baby lying before him and tilted his head to one side, as if trying to understand what was happening. His ears were alert, listening to the quiet sound of the stable. An expression of utter amazement crossed his face and finally, he sat down among the other animals. Nobody seemed bothered by his presence, not even Timothy. Felix looked again at the dormouse, but differently this time. The two seemed to share a moment of mutual understanding. After a few moments, Felix looked at the other gifts lying near the baby. Without a sound, he crept forward and with one paw reached up and slid the jeweled collar over his head and dropped it at the foot of the manger.

Suddenly, Baruch thought of Yonah. If only the dove could see what was happening, he thought. Quietly, he moved to where

Lydia lay and gently pulled the lifeless Yonah from the camel's pack. Tenderly, he laid the dove's lifeless body at the foot of the manger. All of the other animals gathered around.

Baruch wished desperately that the poor dove could see the child. He remembered how Yonah had sacrificed his own life to save Timothy from Felix, how he had inspired the others to search for the King. It was Yonah who had prepared them for this day. But now the valiant bird lay dead. It didn't seem right that he was denied the joy of finding the true King.

He didn't notice it at first, but as Baruch sat hoping that Yonah could somehow be with them, the stable began to grow brighter and brighter. Finally, a light descended directly on the dove and Yonah was bathed in glowing whiteness. He began to move. His eyes opened. His tail fluttered. Baruch wondered in amazement as the dove gathered himself and spread his wings. He flew into the air, circled once and landed on the edge of the King's cradle where he looked lovingly down at the child that he had sacrificed so much to find. Baruch knew in his heart that the child before him was the Son of God.

Baruch wished he could give a gift like each of the other animals had done, but he had nothing to give. He sat for a while longer, thinking to himself. Perhaps he could find something, if he tried. That was it! He would venture out into the city and find a wonderful treasure and then bring it back for the King. He could at least do that much. Quietly, he slipped out of the stable and back into the streets of the city.

33

New Beginning

Baruch trotted down one street and then up another, looking for something fit to give the King. There were still people everywhere and none of them seemed too friendly. More than once he was waved off and an old man even threw a stone at him. The tired faces of the crowds and the cold, harsh streets of the city made him want to be back in the warm glow of the stable with his friends.

Still, Baruch continued to look. For the rest of the night he searched the streets. He was determined to find something fit for the child. He wouldn't give up until he had. On he went.

Baruch was tired. The horizon on the edge of town began to glow a faint pink and in the distance, Baruch heard the distinct sound of a rooster crowing.

As the morning sun began to rise, his hopes began to fade. At last, he lay down beneath the window of a small building. He could hear voices inside and suddenly a man stepped out from the doorway with a basket full of bread. As the man moved across the street, one small loaf fell from the basket and tumbled onto the road. Without noticing, the man continued in the direction of the market. Without hesitation, Baruch leapt to his feet, crossed the street, and carefully picked up the loaf between his teeth. Excited to give his gift, he trotted back toward the stable.

Apparently, he had been away longer than he thought, because when Baruch finally arrived back at the stable, he found that everyone was gone. Sadly, he placed the loaf of bread on the floor and peered into the empty manger. He hadn't made it back in time. Baruch lay down next to the manger, put his chin between his paws and closed his eyes. He had never felt so alone.

"Why are you still here?" a voice asked.

Baruch looked up to see a white dove perched on the edge of the manger. "Yonah?"

"Hello Baruch," the dove responded. "Why haven't you left with the others? Our search for the King is over. He is safe."

"I went to get a gift for the King, but now He is not here," Baruch explained sadly. "Do you know where He has gone?"

"I do," said the dove. "Joseph has been warned that as long as Herod is alive he will seek to destroy the child," explained Yonah. "So Joseph has taken Mary and the child away from Bethlehem. They are on their way to Egypt where the Holy One will be safe until Herod no longer rules over Jerusalem. But we know that someday the King will return to save His people."

"But I was not able to give Him a gift," Baruch sighed.

"You have given Him the greatest gift of all, Baruch. You have given Him your heart. To give of one's self is the most holy gift. Because of you, all of our lives have been blessed as a result of your determination to find the King."

"I don't understand," said Baruch.

"Your gift to the King was helping each of us find our way to the Savior. Because you brought us here to Him, we each have a new beginning. Lydia has joined the other camels and has never been happier. Naomi can lay eggs again, and Ezra welcomed the sun this very morning with his strong voice. Eli wants to return to Jerusalem because he has found new purpose in completing his work at the temple mount. And because you brought me to the King, I too have been given a new life."

"Where will you go now?" asked Baruch.

"I will follow Heber and Joseph as they take Mary and the child to Egypt."

"I want to go with you."

"You must stay here," Yonah replied. "There is more work for you to do."

"What do you mean?" Baruch questioned.

Before the dove could answer, the sound of a goat's gruff voice called from the doorway of the stable. "Are you coming or not?"

Baruch turned to see Ahaz standing nearby with Timothy the dormouse perched on his back.

"Coming where?" the dog asked.

"I'm taking Timothy back to the temple. After that, I'm going to the shepherds' field. You could join me and help protect the sheep," Ahaz said. "You would make a great watchdog, I'll bet they could use someone with a true sense of responsibility."

Baruch turned and spoke to Yonah. "My life is definitely looking up. I think I am beginning to like this ol' goat."

"Well don't get too attached," Ahaz replied.

"I can see the two of you will make a great team," said Yonah lovingly. "Serving others brings the greatest joy of all."

"I guess it's time for us to go," said Timothy.

"Yes," said Yonah. "And I must leave you now."

Baruch took one last look at Yonah. "Goodbye Yonah,"

"Goodbye," Yonah said as he spread his wings and took flight.

Baruch looked at Ahaz and Timothy, and then he turned to watch Yonah fly away.

As the trio topped a small rise in the road, Baruch paused and looked across the fields. In the distance beyond the stable he could see Joseph leading Heber on the road toward Egypt. Heber carried Mary and the Holy Child. Yonah soared high above them. The higher Yonah flew, the brighter he became, until he seemed to be a brilliant ray of light shining in the early morning sky.

Baruch turned to Ahaz who was standing next to him and asked, "Ahaz, are you happy yet?"

"I'm happy," Ahaz answered with a smile.

The End